Finding Wisdom in a Broken World

Audrey-Jane Colson

To:

From:

Published by Pebble in My Shoe Press
Online: findingwisdom.faith

Library of Congress Cataloging-In-Publication Data
Finding wisdom in a broken world / Audrey-Jane Colson—1ˢᵗ ed.
ISBN: 978-0-9978509-0-1
eSBN: 978-0-9978509-1-8

See page 198 for a list of Bible translations used in this book.

Cover design by Brad Gantt

This book is dedicated to my husband Leonard. He has loved, supported and encouraged me through the seasons of plenty and the seasons of lean. We have faced serious illness together, we have laughed and we have cried. We have loved and we have fought but through it all, we've stuck together. He is a man of great integrity and solid principles and simply the finest human being I have ever known. I don't know why he chose me but I am forever grateful he did. This is for you honey, with all my love forever.

When you are eighty years old, and in a quiet moment of reflection narrating for only yourself the most personal version of your life story, the telling that will be the most compact and meaningful will be the series of choices you have made. In the end, we are our choices.

– Jeff Bezos,
founder of Amazon.com
commencement speech
at Princeton University
May 30, 2010

CONTENTS

Finding Wisdom
in a Broken World

FINDING WISDOM
IN A BROKEN WORLD

"If any of you lacks wisdom, let him ask of God who gives to all men liberally and without criticism and it will be given to him." James 1:5 MEV

What exactly is wisdom? Are you wise? Is being smart the same as being wise?

If intelligence is the ability to acquire knowledge, then wisdom is the soundness of decision making with regard to the application of experience, knowledge, good judgment and the persistent use of truth.

The *persistent* use. Wisdom is the understanding that we must choose to base our decisions on what is real and not try to bend reality to fit ourselves.

Intelligence is the ability to absorb knowledge; wisdom is the ability to apply it in a way that will benefit us in the long term, to set aside our short-term gratification and not search for just a good course of action but the best one.

Every day, all day, we make choices. Decision after decision. The big ones get our full attention. We ponder them, mull them over, sometimes obsess over them:

Where will I live?

What shall I study in school?

What kind of work should I do?

Do I want to get married, and if so, do I want a family?

Some choices don't matter much:

Should I buy a blue or a green car?

Should I eat lunch at 12 or 1?

Chicken or fish?

But what about all the decisions that lie in between? The choices that seem small and insignificant, the ones we don't even think about, those governed by our habits, conventional thinking or the current culture?

A meaningful life is made up of millions of choices that, like the principle of compound interest, build upon themselves and over time, spell the difference between success and failure.

I once had a teacher who said, "Education without application is worse than worthless." Worse. What happens when deep down I know which way to go but choose the opposite?

Not only do I suffer the consequences of my poor decision, but since I know I knew better, now I get to keep company with those terrible triplets: regret, guilt and shame.

Wisdom needs to be cultivated at the beginning of any decision process. We need to learn to consistently ask the question, "Is the short-term benefit worth the long- term consequence?" This question just by itself will save us a lot of misery.

Does the acquisition of more knowledge bring us closer to wisdom?

Most of us prize formal education. We look at a person with many years of schooling and a lot of letters after their name and think, they must be very smart, smarter than me, so I should listen to them.

Yes, education is important. Curiosity about the world and how it works is a valuable characteristic to possess. We should accept nothing at face value, we should yearn to learn.

So what is the starting point of wisdom? In today's culture, we are being encouraged to live by our feelings, so should we begin by analyzing how we feel about whatever issue we're facing?

If feelings are a valuable tool to use, why do we make so many mistakes? We can see when decisions based on feelings lead our friends astray, so why can we so easily see the poor choices others are making and yet be blind to our own?

Perhaps, sometimes, our feelings lie to us. They don't hold up as a solid foundation because they tend to shift and change at a moment's notice. A house built on feelings would crumble at even the slightest underground tremor.

Feeling our way to a decision is fraught with danger. Pushing aside reality to suit our mercurial feelings can be disastrous.

But what if I'm doing well? I've trusted my feelings and they haven't let me down so far.

Momentary calm waters don't hold the answer. Many of us appear to be doing just fine and yet, if we dig a little below the surface, we may find that success in one area of life doesn't always translate to success in others.

Why is the CEO of the billion dollar corporation obese?

Why is the brilliant professor on his third marriage?

Why is the powerful politician caught in lie after lie?

Why the disconnect? Could a series of seemingly small choices have lead to a future disaster? Could a search for wisdom have prevented a crushing avalanche?

Our default response often goes like this:

Oh, but you don't understand, I am far too busy to reflect. *I have to keep barreling forward in a never ending effort to keep up with the demands on my time and energy. Quiet reflection and thought are luxuries I can't afford.*

Busyness is prized in our culture. "Want something done? Ask a busy person!" Being busy has become a mark of social status. TV and the internet can make free time just as engaging and isolating as work.

We literally have no time to make calm, rational, prayerful, well thought-out, informed, wise choices because we are so in demand.

There was a man who walked on the Earth about 2000 years ago who made very wise decisions.

Jesus had a great deal to accomplish in his three years of ministry here on earth. In a typical day he would give sight to a blind man or turn water into wine or raise a child from the dead, cast out a few demons, and then preach and teach. His schedule was full and he was interrupted constantly.

Oh and yes, he also had to prepare himself to die on the cross to pay the price for the sins of humankind, past, present and future and then for an encore rise from the dead to live forever, in glory, at the right hand of the father.

And yet, somehow, he was never in a hurry. He had time for the sick, the poor, the needy, the little children, everybody.

I wonder what Jesus saw when he caught a glimpse of his own reflection.

Were his eyes bright or dull? Was his frame lean or pudgy? Was there a spring in his step or did he just shuffle along?

Did he greet people with a smile or did he heave a tired sigh as he geared himself up for yet another request for a miracle? When he opened his eyes in the morning did he thank his father for another day or wonder how he was going to make it through until quitting time?

Was he exhausted or energized? Optimistic or defeated?

Was he making good choices or great ones?

> *"It is absolutely clear that God has called you to a free life. Just make sure that you don't use this freedom as an excuse to do whatever you want to and destroy your freedom." Galatians 5:13 The Message*

Since I won't be raising anyone from the dead today or turning water into wine or giving someone sight, what exactly am I doing that is so important I haven't time to think through my decisions? Am I so busy I forget I even have choices?

Am I running through life as though I was three years old? Do I see something bright and shiny and want it? Do I just go for it?

What do I do when, as a loving earthly parent desires to protect their precious child from harm by saying no to the bright and shiny thing that will hurt them, God says to me: turn away. Stop and turn, pause and let me show you a better way.

How do I pause? How do I stop and listen?

Jesus said, "Love the Lord your God with all your heart, with all your soul, with all your mind and all your strength." Heart? I get that. Soul? No problem. Strength? Yes! But mind? What does it mean to love God with all your mind? Our minds are where the choices in life come alive, the home of our free will.

> *"You say 'I am allowed to do anything' but not everything is good for you. And even though 'I am allowed to do anything' I must not become a slave to anything." 1 Corinthians 6:12 NLT*

This is wisdom in a nutshell, the essence of thinking through the truth of a decision that needs to be made. Will what I am about to do hurt me or harm me? Will it make me free or enslave me? Move me forward or hold me back? Lift me up or tear me down? Give me momentary pleasure followed by long-term misery?

Wise responses to these questions will allow us to thrive in true freedom.

> **"For the reverence and fear of God are basic to all wisdom. Knowing God results in every other kind of understanding." Proverbs 9:10 TLB**

Wisdom is abundant; it is there waiting in every area of our lives. God grants wisdom freely and without restraint. He will give you all you need.

At times it may seem as though it is buried deep, but it isn't. Wisdom is quite easy to find—we just have to stop and look for it. It's there, waiting to be uncovered.

So without judgment or condemnation, let's explore some of the many areas of choice in our daily lives and learn how to ask the questions that will lead us to well considered, prayerful decisions. Let's take wisdom out of the abstract and learn how to begin to apply it in our daily lives, in the way we handle our money and resources, how we grow and nurture our relationships, the care of our bodies and much more.

God longs to shower you with the blessings of his wisdom every day of your life. He has a never ending supply of loving guidance with your name on it, and he's just waiting for you to ask so he can give it to you.

FINDING WISDOM
IN GOD'S WAITING ROOM

Living on the Edge of Expectation

> *"But those who hope in the Lord will renew their strength. They will soar like wings on eagles, they will run and not grow weary, they will walk and not be faint." Isaiah 40:31 NIV*

> *"Yes, wait for and confidently expect the Lord." Psalm 27:14 AMP*

Do you enjoy waiting? Probably not. Even those of us who consider ourselves patient (I don't fit in this category) do not like to wait. And yet waiting is what we do most often in life.

We wait for this, that or the other to begin or end. We wait to finish school. We wait to meet the right "one". We wait all the time, for food in a restaurant, for the red light to change. Our lives are spent waiting for something or someone.

The hardest waiting of all is for God to answer our prayers.

We can pray repeatedly for the same thing and nothing happens. We can get on our knees in tears and agony and nothing happens. We can spend what seems like eternity in a dark night of the soul and nothing happens.

We can have a positive attitude and nothing happens. We can wish really, really hard…and still nothing.

What do we do when we're stuck in the waiting room and we've read all the magazines?

There are two ways to wait. We can wait passively, negatively, for the other shoe to drop.

Or we can wait expectantly, full of hope, knowing at any moment God will move the shadows and we will be bathed in light. We can live on the edge of expectation.

I am very familiar with both methods.

In October, 2008, for the first time in my life, I suddenly got very sick. One morning I woke up out of a deep sleep having difficulty breathing. I had never experienced anything like it. My husband and my best friend, Mary, rushed me to the emergency room and after a battery of tests the official diagnosis was allergy-induced asthma but more than one doctor told me I was an "interesting case," which means we have no idea why you have this.

The drugs I took to relax my airways made me sicker. My nose swelled completely shut and I could barely swallow. I had to sleep sitting up, because if I tried to lay down, it made my breathing worse. I was terrified and exhausted all the time. I was living a nightmare. My breathing would calm for a few hours and then I would be hit with another attack. Day after week after month.

I went to an allergist who, after more tests, said I was allergic to one thing: a certain kind of tree. And this particular tree didn't grow anywhere near our house. I was sent home with more drugs and told to rest. I couldn't do anything but.

In January 2009 I was watching the presidential inauguration on television and I saw a pastor I had never heard of, Rick Warren, give the invocation prayer. I had never heard of him. It turned out he had written a rather popular book. I asked my husband, Leonard, to go and buy it for me. When I read the introduction to *The Purpose Driven Life* I decided to do as it instructs and read one chapter a day for 40 days. I asked Leonard to read it with me and he agreed.

For the first time in my life I began to realize that being a Christian, a follower of Christ, was not about religion or dogma or other manmade rules. It was about a relationship with my creator. I slowly began to understand that God created me for a purpose and loved me beyond all reason and he knew what was best for me in every aspect of my life —my decisions, my relationships, my lifestyle, everything.

One night, the true meaning of despair became very clear to me. All alone, I hit rock bottom. Up until that moment, I didn't understand what despair was. Suddenly it was no longer an abstract concept but a real, true, deep feeling that overwhelmed every part of me. I simply had no more fight left. I dropped the last vestige of control I had been holding onto so tightly and it fell with a thud. I turned away from myself and looked up. To Jesus. And he welcomed me, with arms wide open, into his world. Something in my heart cracked.

I have never been the same. *When I willingly gave up my life I finally, at last, began to find it.*

Little by little I stopped looking to myself for answers and looked to God. It takes time to break old habits and unhealthy ways of thinking and I had plenty of both. I began to learn how to pray, to speak to God as someone who loved me, who accepted me, who observed me to my very core and who was interested in every tiny aspect of my existence.

Since he knew me better than I knew myself and was rooting for me to win, I asked him to show me his path and to help me stay on it. I sought wisdom in his Word. I looked for ways to get to know him better.

Do you know what it is like to know that your heavenly father *knows* you, every last little detail, and loves you beyond your ability to understand?

> **"Jesus is just so awesome. I wish the whole world knew what intimacy with him is like."**
> **–Eileen Heuston**

More than anything, I want you to know Jesus, too.

And so I began to reveal myself in honesty and trust. Even though I knew he knows my heart, I had to learn how to be authentic and transparent before him and before myself. I had to learn to tear away old pretenses and masks. For some of us, that's not easy.

I started keeping a journal. Every day, sometimes more than once, I wrote letters to God. I told him the truth, I didn't hold back. I cried out to him, literally. I cried a lot.

I found promises in the Bible and and inserted my name for the pronouns.

Instead of "I can do all things through Christ who gives me strength" (Philippians 4:13), I said, "Audrey-Jane can do all things through Christ who gives her strength." Sometimes I spoke these words choking on tears.

And I started to realize that, through his Word, God was talking to *me*. I learned more about his character, about who he is, that he is a good, good father, the one I never had.

Little by little I began to feel better about myself. I learned for the first time, who I am, a beloved child of God, not some multi-generational accident as I had often felt. I began to see my place in this world.

But the illness remained. I didn't get well; in fact I got worse. I spent hours and hours on the internet looking for methods of healing. I tried many things, including a 40-day juice fast (yes, just water and fresh juice) and I lost a lot of weight. Over the course of my illness I lost the 40 pounds I had needed to lose all my adult life, and which I have kept off to this day. In the midst of all my misery, there was a gift.

At night, sitting on the sofa in our sunroom, I watched

archived sermons, Pastor Rick's and others. I did video small-group studies and devotionals by myself. I even joined an online small group through Saddleback Church, which later became my church family.

Every few weeks I would have an okay day or two and think I was starting to get better, and then, wham, right back down.

I would like to tell you I never had a pity party, but it's not true. The days were long and endless. I thought, well, my life is over. During the parties I would think, one day I will have a massive asthma attack and suffocate and that will be it. But I wasn't afraid. I was, at times, resigned, but not afraid.

I used to sob in Leonard's arms, saying that although God could heal me—and I truly believed he could—for some reason he was choosing not to. I cried out to the Lord and he did, indeed, send me comfort. He did, indeed, calm my spirit, But I would wake up the next day, still sick.

God knew me so well, the good, the bad, the indifferent, and he didn't let go. He had a plan. When the time was right, he would show it to me. *In the meantime, he had something to teach me, something I could learn in no other way and under no other circumstances.*

I learned that when worry came to visit, I could decide to worship instead. Instead of feeling sorry for myself, I could thank God for all he was giving me every day. Yes, I was sick. Yes, I felt like crap most of the time, pretty much all the time. But at the same time, there were many, many blessings in my life, too. I could choose to focus more on them.

I could choose to look upward instead of inward. I could look into my circumstances or look up to Jesus. And that choice made all the difference.

And so I didn't give up. I kept seeking God. And as I sought him, he revealed his power in a thousand little ways. The more I let him carry me, the calmer I got. Finally the pity parties stopped.

At last, after 18 months, I started to feel better. The swelling in my nose subsided and I was able to breathe through it and as a result my bronchial tubes started to relax and I was able, slowly, to resume a normal life.

The time I spent in God's waiting room changed my life forever. He knew exactly the perfect set of circumstances and exactly the right kind of experiences I needed to become the woman he created me to be.

He loved me so much and wanted me so badly he was willing to let me suffer to be sanctified.

Then, barely a month after I began living again, Leonard injured his back. Badly. He could barely move. You see, God was calling him, too. And for the first time in his life, he was weak. He could do nothing. Flat on his back he had nowhere to look but up. And he reached up and Jesus was there. He always is. *Leonard gave up his life too, and began, for the first time, to find it. He has never been the same, either.*

Fast forward four years.

Late in 2013 I got sick again. I had strange symptoms that

would come and go, not breathing problems this time but debilitating pain, weakness and fatigue. Again, I was an interesting case.

As before, weeks and months went by and I felt no better. Then I fell and broke my wrist, requiring surgery. I was exhausted and miserable.

But this time something was different. I knew God was going to bring something good out of my suffering, I just knew it. I chose to hold God to his promises. I chose to believe he was working in a powerful way in my life even if I couldn't see it right then. I told him—and I meant it—that I didn't want to get better if it meant going back to any of my old bad habits or poor ways of thinking. I willingly submitted to the sanding of my rough edges. I didn't fight him.

With Jesus beside me, loving me, encouraging me and giving me his strength I made it through.

The book you are reading is a result of the mighty power of God working through me.

He has a beautiful plan for you, too.

His waiting room is where you will go to university, where you will receive a master's degree in patience, in perseverance and in overcoming fear. It is where you will learn that:

> *"My grace is all you need. My power works best in weakness." 2 Corinthians 12:9 NLT*

It does, indeed. Pastor Rick always says, "You don't know God is all you need until God is all you've got."

If you are in God's waiting room right now, stop digging through the magazines looking for a momentary distraction.

Don't let another hour go by without speaking the truth of your heart, mind and spirit to the Lord. Tell him just how bad you feel. Give details. Tell him if you are angry, if you are afraid, if your faith is shaky. He can take it. Don't hold back anything.

Ask him to reveal to you any part of your being that is out of sync with him. Repent in true humility. As the Lord convicts your heart, turn away from anything he tells you to.

> *"And we know (with great confidence) that God (who is deeply concerned about us) causes all things to work together (as a plan) for good for those who love God, to those who are called to his plan and purpose." Romans 8:28 AMP*

I chose the Amplified Bible translation of this well known verse for a reason.

When we love God, when we trust him, when we obey, when we repent and turn away from sin, we are assured of a great plan for our lives no matter how twisted our circumstances, no matter how hopeless they may appear. God is not bound as we are by time and space, by mere human understanding. We see only our past, usually muddled with regrets and guilt, and our present, often a mass of confusion as well.

God sees everything clearly. He knows precisely the

schooling I need to be equipped for the career he is calling me to. Sometimes the curriculum will involve pain and suffering, but I will emerge with a knowing assurance I have never had before.

It takes four years to complete high school, another four years for an undergraduate degree, another year or two for a master's and six or more for a PhD.

Those years are spent focusing almost exclusively on the chosen field of endeavor. Much sacrifice is required way beyond the obvious time and money. *And waiting with great expectation is necessary.*

But in the end, we are equipped to go forth into the world with the education needed to succeed, at least that is what we hope.

The difference between earthly school and the University of God is that in his college we have complete assurance that, if we do the work required, not only will we graduate, but we are assured of great success. There is a goal, a plan, a future, waiting for us that is good and will succeed.

No human school can give us that guarantee.

If you align yourself with God's plan, he will work out everything in your life for good. You are called, you are chosen, you are picked for the greatest career of all. There is absolutely nothing better. Nothing.

So study hard. Listen well. Talk to your professor often. While you are waiting, learn everything you can.

Live on the edge of expectation for your graduation day; it will be here sooner than you think.

Your gown has been pressed. The tassel has been attached to your cap.

And your diploma has already been signed.

FINDING WISDOM
IN MY HOPES AND DREAMS

"For we are God's handiwork, created in Christ Jesus to do good works which God prepared in advance for us to do." Ephesians 2:10 NIV

Prepared in advance. You mean God has already prepared a plan for my life?

Yes. Your life plan has already been written. God has given you a dream, a hope for something he wants you to do and the method for achieving it. The problem is, many of us don't look to God for guidance; we think we can figure out the steps by ourselves.

All of us carry around deep longing for something. We want to get married, have kids, an exciting career, perhaps to travel. We desire something, maybe many things.

When our dreams don't materialize on our timetable we get impatient, we stamp our feet: "Okay, God, I'm ready. Let's get started!"

But God says, "Wait, it isn't time yet." Or worse, "No, that is not the dream I have planned for you to fulfill. I know you think it is the best, but I have something better."

What we think is a dead end may be the key to launching the biggest, most fulfilling dream of our lives.

One of the most important words our parents ever said to us was no. It is exactly the same with our heavenly father.

As our three-year-old selves, we want what we want when we want it. We don't see the beginning, the middle and the end as God does. We see only what is right in front of us.

God knows very well the deepest desires of our hearts. He also knows the plan he has for us, a plan perfectly tailored to our particular gifts, personality and experience. And through his plan, God will use us in miraculous ways.

But like a child, we often don't care what God wants.

"I want to go play in the street!" "But if you go in the street you will get hurt." " I don't care!" "But I *do* care," says the Lord.

Many of our prayers are centered on asking God to bless what we are doing and to give us what we want, at least what we think we want. Have you ever reached a goal only to find emptiness in the achievement? Have you ever thought, I don't know what I want?

We all have. So instead, what if we opened our hearts and hands to God and then actively looked for opportunities to serve others, glorify him and build the kingdom?

How would that change our outlook on the present and the future? How would our limited perspective expand?

Now you may be thinking, I don't want to give up my hopes and dreams. I still want what I want. Surely God isn't against me getting married or having kids or a career in which I can glorify him.

Of course not. The problem comes when we focus on what we want to the exclusion of what God wants for us. Our human nature always leads in the direction of "me" where God wants us to move in the direction of "him".

There is a simple way to set yourself in alignment with God: listen to him speak to you through his Word. Read the following verse carefully.

> *"Now to him who is able to do immeasurably more than all we ask or imagine, according to His power that is at work within us, to Him be the glory."*
> *Ephesians 3:20 NIV*

Now read it again. One more time.

According to his power that is at work within us…more than all we ask or imagine.

So, are you telling me that with God's power at work within me, I will receive more than I ask for? Beyond my wildest dreams?

Yes.

When we put God at the center of everything we do, when we immerse ourselves in his Word, surround ourselves with his people, worship him constantly both alone and with others, he gives us the ability to tap into his boundless strength and power. Our perspective begins to shift and we begin to see ourselves differently, not so much as "mine" but more as "his". Me, myself, I can do very little. He can do *anything*.

I have hopes and dreams, and so do you. But our hopes, dreams, and aspirations are puny compared to what God has in mind for my life and for yours. He made us. He loves us. He wants us to grow and flourish and be all he created us to be. Yes, he wants us to reach our full potential. And you know what? We have absolutely no idea what that even is... **but he does**.

How exciting is that? We have the opportunity to play a part in the greatest project ever undertaken, the building of the kingdom of God, which, unlike any human culture or society, will never end. God is calling his people to join him. He is calling you.

Your hopes and dreams may not work out the way you planned but they will be replaced with something greater, more joyful, more fulfilling than you can conceive of because God's dream for you will never end. He is patiently waiting to put it to work in your life. He is quietly knocking on your door, inviting you to come and join the party. What are you waiting for?

Your plan is okay His plan is phenomenal. And you don't want to miss out, do you?

"If God were small enough for your mind, he wouldn't be big enough for your needs."
—Greg Laurie

FINDING WISDOM
IN DISCERNING MY CALLING

Trust and obey,
For there's no other way
To be happy in Jesus
But to trust and obey

(Trust and Obey
Music by Daniel Towner
Lyrics by John Sammis)

"If we do not pray, then we only accomplish the sum
total of our own abilities." –Buddy Owens

Some people just seem to know what they were called to do in life. I have a friend who is a speech pathologist. When she was a small child she needed speech therapy and she loved it so much she made up her mind that was what she was going to do when she grew up. And she did. She loves her work and is content with her choice.

But what about the rest of us? What if I like a lot of things?

What if I am good at more than one thing? How do I discern what God wants for my life?

In the body of Christ we all have a purpose, a role designed just for us. There is a place we fit in; there is plenty of work to be done. There are tasks we are perfectly shaped to carry out.

Not everything we enjoy is part of our calling. I enjoy music, but no one is going to ask me to sing! But I use my enjoyment of music to worship God, which brings me closer to him.

God knows exactly what he wants us to do. The rub is we often think we have a better plan. The pot wants to tell the potter what it was designed for.

Instead, what if we started with an attitude of submission and went before our creator with an open and humble mind and asked for guidance. What if we refused to hurry or put pressure on ourselves? What if we opened our hearts and minds and allowed him to steer them in the direction he knows is best? What if we were still and quiet and listened with a faithful, expectant posture?

What if, instead of asking God to bless my plan, my idea, my goal, I asked him to allow me to participate in his plan for my life? What if I asked to be a part of what he is blessing?

My idea is formed from only what I can see. I have no true vision of what it could become. I can formulate a plan and have a positive attitude, but ultimately I have no idea what will happen, whether I will meet with success or failure. I have no guarantee of the outcome.

However, God's idea, his plan for my life, is perfectly thought out and perfectly planned. He knows exactly what to do with the work he has for me, how it will impact the world, how it will help build his kingdom. I just need to get on board and trust him.

Trust and obedience are the keys to discerning God's will, trusting that he loves me and has a perfect plan for me, obeying even when I don't understand everything I face in life, but still continuing to believe he is faithful and will bless me if I trust that he knows best and keep following where he is leading.

God's plan is often revealed slowly. He knows exactly how much we can handle. If he revealed the whole scheme at once, with all the work involved, the trials and tribulations along the way, most of us would run because the task would seem too daunting. But God knows, that with his almighty power working within us, we can do it.

So he starts a little at a time. He uses people and events to build our faith. He gives small rewards along the way. In revealing himself and his power in small doses he grows our trust.

God backs up his promises with rewards to show us he is faithful and trustworthy, a father who keeps his word.

Sometimes rewards come right away. And sometimes they don't.

When his time frame doesn't meet ours, we go before God and, like a questioning child, ask, "okay, I trusted you, I cleaned my room, now where's my ice cream?"

God's plan is so complex and so perfect, often it is only in hindsight that we see how the pieces fit together. But God, in his infinite love has given us guideposts, signs to follow along the way. They are found in the owner's manual for life.

There are thousands of promises and assurances in the Bible, covenants that God makes with us if we will simply obey his rules. These rules have one purpose: to keep us from harm. Every time I claim one of these promises for myself, I trust God a little bit more and I begin to see, with new eyes, how he is working in my life.

I used to struggle with sensing God's presence. I read my Bible every day. I prayed, I went to church and Bible study every week and still, most of the time, God seemed very far away. In my head I believed he was close but I rarely felt him in my heart. A part of me still wanted to do things my way.

But slowly, as I began to obey, to move away from the enticing things of the world that were distracting me, I began to sense him at work inside of me. As I began to embrace the fruit of the spirit (Galatians 5:22-23), I asked him to reveal the parts of me that were out of alignment with him, and he certainly did! The more I obeyed, the more I trusted, the more he showed himself to me, the clearer my calling became.

People began to appear in my path to teach me what he wanted me to learn. The wisdom of the Bible became clearer and more understandable. I became aware of the areas in my life where sin still had a stronghold, and it became easier to let go of the things that were holding me back. I have been given the spiritual gift of discernment, which is great, but the flip side is my tendency to be very judgmental. I would judge people all the time and find them wanting. Or I would compare myself to others and come out either way behind or way ahead. Whichever end I landed on, I wasn't honoring the person God created because I was always preoccupied with what other people were doing.

As I immersed myself in the Bible, as I spent more and more time in pursuit of the truth of who I was in God's eyes, a miracle took place. As I began to find my identity in Christ, as I began to recognize and confess to the Lord the many little sins swirling around me all the time, repenting and then moving forward, lifelong insecurities and low self-esteem vanished as I was reminded, by his promises, of just who I really am.

I am a precious, unique, one-of-a-kind, loved-beyond-all-reason, child of the living God.

And so are you. When we find our identity in Christ it changes everything.

I began to realize he had my calling all figured out and was just waiting for me to make the decision to join him. Once I understood that, I couldn't wait to get started!

And you know what? Obedience got a whole lot easier. As I trusted and obeyed, God continued to reveal his power to me. He began to open doors; he began to multiply the gifts he gave me as I used them for his purpose and his glory. *The proof is in the words you are reading.*

When I trust God, when I obey him, I see his power and

strength. As he dominates every area of my life, he reveals himself to me. When I worship him for who he is, I feel his love. I want to clean my room because of the blessed assurance I have that he will do as he says. He will give me the rewards he promised because he cannot be unfaithful, it is simply not in his character.

Sometimes the ice cream doesn't arrive right away, but when it does, boy is it yummy!

So how do we get started?

> "Do not conform to the pattern of this world but be transformed by the renewing of your mind. Then you will be able to test and approve what God's will is—his good, pleasing, perfect will." Romans 12:2 NIV

What does it mean to renew your mind? Look around at all the areas of your life. Have you put God at the center of each? Does Jesus reside in every room in your house? Does he travel with you? Is he with you at work?

Or are some doors still closed to him?

When you accepted Jesus as your Lord and Savior, were you changed?

The great Christian philosopher and apologist William Lane Craig says it this way: "Examine yourself to insure that when you trusted Christ you received his Holy Spirit. Sometimes one senses a new life within; other times people may sense the change in you before you sense it yourself. Why is the presence of the Holy Spirit so crucial? Simply because we are spiritually dead apart from him. When the Holy Spirit comes into you, you can know and experience God."

The Holy Spirit is God in a form I can handle. God is so powerful with pure love I cannot take him in. Jesus is so bright with pure love I cannot look upon him. But I can sense the Holy Spirit inside me, guiding me, making God's Word clearer to me. I can feel the presence of the Advocate. He calms me. He energizes my determination. He keeps me centered.

God's number one rule is that I put him first in everything, in every area of my life. He is a jealous God because he knows that, left to my own devices, I am headed for trouble.

> *"You shall have no other gods before me."*
> *Exodus 20:3 MEV*

The word *jealous,* when used to describe God, means he is determined to protect what is most precious to him: you and me.

God demands he be first in our lives because he understands our human limitations. We are like sheep: left on our own we will meander around in a circle and eventually off a cliff. We will search endlessly for meaning in life and never find it because true meaning is only found in Christ.

As long as I freely give my hopes and dreams and plans to God, they are alive and limitless. He will multiply my talents and abilities beyond my wildest imagination.

When I choose to hold on tightly to them, they may or may not succeed, but even if they do, it will only be within the limitations of my human ability, and that is nothing compared to what God can do.

Want to discern God's calling for your life?

Let go of yours.

FINDING WISDOM
IN HUMILITY AND TRUST

"God opposes the proud but gives grace to the humble. So humble yourselves under the mighty power of God and at the right time he will lift you up in honor. Give all your worries and cares to God for he cares about you." 1 Peter 5:5b-7 NIV

or put another way:

"God has had it with the proud. But he takes delight in plain people. So be content with who you are and don't put on airs. God's strong hand is on you; he'll promote you at the right time. Live carefree before God, he is most careful with you."
The Message

Live carefree…he is most careful…

What are we most careful with? Kids, of course. Anyone who has ever been around children knows safety comes first.

Often children don't know what will harm them, but as we grow, we learn what to avoid and pass our knowledge on to younger ones.

Children of good, loving parents don't worry much about being hurt because they know someone bigger is looking out for them. Even though they may really, really want to touch the hot stove, and maybe they will, after the tears have dried they can rest assured that their mom and dad are still there to protect them.

My friend Elodie is all grown up. It has been more than a few years since she was a child. Recently she gave her life to Jesus and she told me something very interesting.

She said she finally came to Jesus because she was exhausted. She had been doing all the right things. She attended church; she served on various volunteer projects; she helped feed the needy. She talked about God; she prayed; she read her Bible. She *did* all the right things. But deep inside she was still relying on herself, on her intellect and fortitude, to figure out how to live her life, and she was getting nowhere fast.

Now she tells me she is like a child. She looks up to God (he is so much taller than she) and says, "You are my heavenly daddy. You show me what is best. I am just a kid and I have no idea what to do. You tell me what is good and you tell me what is harmful. Left to my own devices I will touch the hot stove again and I am tired of getting burned."

In her childlike humility she has found the answer.

On the cross, Jesus, in three words gave us the secret to life: *It is finished*.

He paid our debt. He took away Satan's power over us. He defeated death. It is *done*.

Now all of us—you, me, Elodie, no exceptions—can live in true freedom. We can be kids again, trusting, carefree and joyful. Those of us who had poor earthly parenting can have the best daddy of all. He is never grumpy, he is never too tired to listen to us and he has the best book of bedtime stories ever written.

You don't have to be strong. You don't have to figure it all out yourself. Your daddy is right there for you. You don't have to do anything, just accept his gift of salvation and you will instantly belong in his family. He is ust waiting for you to come home and climb into his lap for a cuddle.

> **"Heart-shattered lives ready for love don't for a moment escape God's notice." Psalm 51:17 The Message**

FINDING WISDOM
IN FRIENDSHIP

"When three of Job's friends heard of the tragedy he had suffered, they got together and traveled from their homes to comfort and console him."
Job 2:11a NLT

"There is no greater way to love than to give your life for your friends." John 15:13 The Voice

"So many people are living for likes while longing for love." –Craig Groeschel

What is a friend, exactly? I know people who have hundreds of "friends" on social media. Are they really? What does it mean to be "friended'?

Today if we have a Facebook page and a zillion friends, we are viewed as popular and well liked. It is easy to get into the habit of skipping emails and rushing to see how many "likes" we have today. We love that momentary rush of getting attention and feeling important and, (we might think anyway), loved.

Genuine friendship takes a great deal of time and energy. If we sleep a third of our lives and spend another third working and then spend hours surfing the net and engaging with our followers and friends, where do face-to- face, one-on-one relationships fit in?

Are we spending so much time building vast amounts of connections that we have no time left to deepen the ones we already have?

Recently, an acquaintance of mine suffered some serious business and financial reversals. He posted online the details of what happened and received, as of the time I am writing this, 30 plus comments full of "sorries" and various canned platitudes from his Facebook friends. I read his post and comments with great sadness. These verbal pats on the back were what was passing for sympathy and caring. I felt like crying.

Aristotle, in his classic work *Ethics,* said, "A friend is another self." Those are powerful words. Our greatest opportunity for growth is found in our relationships. True meaning in life is found in our bond with God and others.

Aristotle also reminded us, "The desire for friendship comes quickly. Friendship does not."

We are chasing after quick connections. It is so much easier to hit the 'like" button for a fast hit of "how supportive am I" than to enter into another person's world and perhaps into their pain.

I want a friend, I need a friend, but how do I find one? The old cliche is true: the best way to find a friend is to be one.

Go before the Lord and ask him to bring exactly the right people into your path to be blessed by him through you.

Start making eye contact and smiling at people. If you ask someone how they are, actually listen to the answer. If something stands out, ask a followup question. If they share something personal, make a mental note and inquire about it the next time you see them. Tell them you will pray for them and then do it. If they tell you about something they are struggling with or a hurt in their heart that is so very painful, stop and pray for them right then and there.

Little by little, over time, relationships will begin to grow. Water them, fertilize them, respect their dormant seasons and enjoy their blooms. Pray with your friends, lift them up to the Lord, hug them often.

Not everyone you meet will become your friend. My friend Mary, who has been my closest friend for 40-plus years, has friends literally all over the world. She says she can't handle any more friends because she devotes so much time and energy to the ones she has! She never forgets a birthday; she sends cards for no reason, just for encouragement or to say she is thinking of you. In a world of email and texting, an actual paper card sent via snail mail can make someone's day.

Social media does have its place, but it will never replace human contact. Don't make it into something it isn't. Don't isolate yourself behind the computer-be brave and reach out. Yes, you may be rejected, not everyone will welcome your offer of friendship. But there is someone out there waiting for you, someone God has designed to get you and for you to get.

Don't keep them waiting. *A year from now you may call them your friend.*

FINDING WISDOM
IN THE FINE ART OF LISTENING

"Therefore encourage each other and build each other up…" 1 Thessalonians 5:11a NIV

"Being heard is so close to being loved that for the average person they are almost indistinguishable." –David Augsburger

What do you think many of us want, need and fervently desire? It's not a thing. It's not money.

The greatest, most precious, most needed and scarcest commodity in our society today is focused, active *listening*.

A psychologist I know told me many people enter therapy just to have someone listen to them. They will pay simply to be heard.

What often passes for conversation these days goes like this: I talk about me, then you talk about you, then me, then you, then me, then you. Or we endlessly discuss politics or sports or sadly, we gossip.

Charming, well liked people are often spoken of like this: he/she made me feel as though I was the most important person in the room. Because you know, at that moment, you were.

We all struggle with our human tendency to be self absorbed. A relentless search for self-actualization and self-fulfillment leads to ever greater emptiness, loneliness and isolation.

Jesus said it succinctly: "love God, love others". Shut off the chatter in your head and listen. Don't just hear the words, listen to the tone, look at the facial expressions and the body language of the person in front of you.

Everyone, and I mean everyone, we encounter is struggling with something. Life runs on a parallel track. Even in the good times there is pain. The cracks in our broken world are getting deeper.

Listening isn't fixing. It isn't an opportunity to give advice, and it most empathically is not an opportunity to puff yourself up by advising someone to do what worked for you. They are not you.

The very act of focused, attentive listening forces us to step out of ourselves and enter into another person's reality, their joy, their pain. It is a priceless opportunity to look first to God and then into another's heart and extend a healing tonic like no other.

Reaching out in love and truly listening leads to a fullness of spirit that rests in the very depths of our beings.

Along with active listening comes the chance to encourage. Everybody needs encouragement, everyone.

The very act of saying:

I appreciate _____ about you.

I like _____ about you.

I am thankful for _____ about you.

I love _____ about you.

rains down a blessing on the giver and receiver alike that is life changing.

In 2012 and 2013 Leonard and I had the privilege of spending almost a year in Paris. We went on a mission trip to assist two churches with various projects. During the weeks before we left we prayed without ceasing, "Lord, please bring people into our paths who you can bless through us and help us recognize them when you do."

Well, be careful what you ask for! God blessed us richly by bringing literally dozens of people to us.

When people are living in a foreign country they tend to form relationships with people from their homeland or who at least speak their language. Everyone is looking for connection and a place to belong. Many nonbelievers come to church simply to meet people. Outside of the projects we worked on, most of my time was spent listening, one on one, to women I had just met. They told me the most personal things, sharing their fears, their pain, their hopes and dreams.

Now I must stop right here and tell you I am one of those people who used to reside full time in the kingdom of me. As an only child I never had to share my toys and nobody ever messed up my room. I was the queen of my domain.

In school I learned superficial social skills, but they remained just that: superficial. I could have a polite, meaningless conversation with the best of them, but besides my husband, the only person I was close to was Mary, my dearest friend.

I was never an advice giver because people bored me. If someone started rambling on about their problems I found a way to get out quick.

Then something changed. As I grew to know Jesus I began to see the hurt all around me. I began, slowly, to see people the way he does, and true empathy began to take root in my heart for the first time ever. I grew to willingly enter into another person's pain.

And this is what I started hearing: "Audrey-Jane, you are such a good listener." "You actually care about me." "I feel as though I can trust you and I barely know you."

Nobody was more surprised by this than me. When I try and tell someone how I used to be, they shake their heads and say they just can't imagine it.

That is the life-changing power of Jesus Christ.

You see, he listened to me. And he sent Leonard and Mary to listen to me, too. They listened for years and always gave me gallons of grace. I am forever grateful.

The next time you have the opportunity to meet with a friend, pray first. Ask God to open your heart to what he wants you to hear, how he wants to use you to be a blessing. Ask the Holy Spirit to fill you with the right words to say, not too many, just the right amount.

Then sit down, face to face. Turn off your phones. Ask your friend what is going on in their heart. What current boulder are they pushing uphill? What decisions are they facing? What are they joyful about? You'll know what to ask. Then just be quiet and listen.

As they talk, ask gentle questions to draw them out, and speak quietly with words of love and encouragement. Affirm what is good, gently admonish what is troubling and always, always, remind them they are a precious, unique, one-of-a-kind, ravishingly loved-by-the-king of the universe...*child of God*.

Don't let the week go by without having listened to and encouraged someone in need.

And remember: It is far, far better to be interested than to be interesting.

FINDING WISDOM
WITH EGR PEOPLE

Extra Grace Required

> *"Always be humble and gentle. Be patient with each other, making allowance for each other's faults because of your love." Ephesians 4:2 NLT*

> *Every one of us wears an invisible sign on our foreheads: Make Me Feel Important*

Leonard works in children's ministry, mostly with preschoolers. There are always a few kids that need a little extra grace, whether they are crying because Mommy is leaving, or they haven't yet learned how to share, or maybe they're just having a bad day.

When he comes home and tells me stories about the kids, I am always amazed at the way he is able to calm the criers and get the uncooperative to cooperate and to help turn a frown upside down.

Here is his secret: he makes each of them a valuable part of the group. He will ask the shy kid to show him how to assemble the train tracks. He tells the crier he needs help with a project and could they please assist him.

He looks carefully at the ones who are acting out to see if he can discern the cause. Sometimes he can't figure out the problem, but he shows great love and patience to the kids who are hurting and expressing their pain in the only way they know how.

Funny how these kids are just like us. Many of them are hurt and angry and misbehave out of pure frustration.

We do, too. Sometimes we can control ourselves better, sometimes not. Many of us have learned to grit our teeth and white knuckle our not so pleasant feelings. At times, just like kids, we don't want to share, we don't want to think about others. We want it to be *all about me*. What patience we have is forced and easily lost.

I am describing people all around us. At times, maybe like you. Maybe like me.

Until we arrive at our final destination, where there will be no more anger or frustration or tears, here is a tip for dealing with the "other guy" when you are having a good day and he isn't. It also works the other way around:

Wounded people wound people.
The bloodiest wounds are the ones you can't see

Broken people break people.

Some of us are so broken we can barely move.

Crushed people crush people.
Some of us are carrying such a heavy load we are caving
under the weight.

BUT

Wounded people can bind the wounds of others.

Broken people can learn to mend breaks.

Crushed people can rebuild what is smashed and looks
unrepairable.

The name for this is *grace*.

When we feel God's grace, we are encouraged and valued.
The urge to lash out or strike back fades away. When our
hearts are calm and secure we are slow to react. We pause
and think before we speak. And our anger simply dissolves.

God has abundant grace to share. He uses us—broken,
wounded, even crushed, just as we are—to extend his grace
to others.

At times I am an EGR person, who needs extra grace.
Perhaps you are, too.

God has more than enough grace for all of us—we just have
to ask. The more we ask, the more we will receive and the
more we will have to share. And without even realizing it,
grace will take on a life of its own. The more the pump is

primed, the faster the water will flow like a river through our lives and into everyone we touch.

The world is in desperate need of grace. Try sending some out today and see what happens.

FINDING WISDOM
IN BEING ON MY OWN

"And surely I am with you always, to the very end of the age." Matthew 28:20b NIV

Loneliness is part of the human condition. We all yearn for connection, for companionship, for the gentle understanding of another person. We all want someone to get us.

The loneliest place on earth can be in a crowd, surrounded by people I don't know and who don't care about me.

Loneliness is very, very painful. When we are in the pit we cry out, why? Why don't I have a husband, a wife, a child, a friend, a loving family? Why?

We have all felt alone, confined in solitary isolation. But, as when we are in God's waiting room, loneliness can open our eyes and help us see that, although we may be lonely, we are never alone.

I have a friend, Linda, who lives by herself. She has been divorced for many years and her only child lives far away. She has many friends and leads a full life. She is retired from a career in the diplomatic service and spends time each week volunteering at her church and local community center.

As with any single person, she experiences times of loneliness. She doesn't have a man in this season of her life and would love to be married again.

We were talking one day about loneliness and how so many people feel disconnected from God and others. She said something that made me stop in my tracks.

With the sweetest confidence in her voice, she said, "I share my meals with my favorite companion."

When it is time to eat, she prepares her meal, sets the table with a tablecloth and napkin, and sits down to dine. She prays, thanking God for the abundant blessings he gives her, and as she eats she reads her Bible or an inspirational book. She eats slowly, savoring her food and simply relaxing.

She keeps her Bible on her dining room table because, to her, that table is a symbol of where we gather to spend time with the people we love, where we talk and laugh and share the good and the bad.

Relationships grow and flourish around meals taken together. She has kept her Bible on the table for 25 years and she knows Jesus joins her at every meal.

Then we talked about how people are often given Bibles in hospitals and prisons. Again she said something that brought me up short, "You're never alone when you have the Bible."

I think Linda is on to something.

When we feel alone, when it seems as though God is far away, it isn't he who has moved, it's us. We forget that the Holy Spirit resides in our hearts and never leaves.

A beloved pastor in my church talked one day about being in the deserts of life. He said he had gone through a very difficult and painful season and had spent more time than he normally does talking with God and reading his Word.

As the fog finally began to clear and he began to see his way out of the desert and into the richness of life once again, he felt sad. He told Jesus, "I got to know you so much better than I ever have, and I enjoyed your company so much that, as I return to the tasks you have set before me, I will miss our time together. I know you have work for me to do, and I am gladly moving forward, but I will treasure our time together in the desert for the rest of my life."

Wow. He was, in essence, thanking God for the trial, the pain, the loneliness. He was sad to leave because it meant he would lose the sweet connection with his best friend.

So when you are sad, when you are lonely, when your prayers are going unanswered, when you feel the whole world bearing down and have no one to turn to, no one who will listen, no one who gets you, what do you do?

First, recognize that God *is* with you and *he gets you*. It doesn't matter if you don't feel his presence—he is still there. He is attentive and focused on you; he is the best listener ever.

Call a meeting with him; he will show up. Tell him how you feel; don't hold back. It's okay to whine a little. Loneliness can reduce us all to children again.

Ask him what he wants you to do. Ask if you're putting something ahead of him. Have you set an idol before him, your work, your hobbies, even your church? Are you filling your time with meaningless distractions to mitigate your loneliness and to avoid the still small voice telling you that you need to repent of your sin?

Ask the Lord whether it is time to replace a passion, a driver in your life with something new. Where are you needed to serve right now? And tomorrow? And the next day? Who needs your special brand of love and encouragement?

Picture Jesus holding out his hand to you and clasp it. Allow gratitude to fill your heart. Loneliness can be so overwhelming that we can lose sight of all the things we have to be grateful for. The simple act of giving thanks can change sadness into joy.

This side of heaven, we will all feel lonely at times. We will long for unity and a place to fit in.

On Earth we have such a place. It is called the church. It is where deep, lifelong connections are made with our brothers and and sisters in Christ. It is where, in true fellowship, we can be our authentic selves. It is where selfless caring abounds. It is where lasting community is built. And more than anything, it is where hope is found.

Find a church and join it. Don't just attend, join. Become an active member and pretty soon you will find your place. The church will outlast all cultures and governments; it will never end. And it needs you. Now.

No, it won't be perfect, because churches are made up of imperfect people. That's the beautiful part—your brokenness and imperfection will be accepted and embraced. And you will learn how to accept and embrace others, too.

So…go. Volunteer. Smile. Greet. Hug. Listen.

And your loneliness will be replaced with joy, not fleeting happiness, but the joy that comes from loving God, loving others and actively playing your special role in building the kingdom.

There is nothing quite like it.

> *"But as for me, how good it is to be near God! I have made the Sovereign Lord my shelter and I will tell everyone about the wonderful things you do."*
> *Psalm 73:28 NLT*

FINDING WISDOM
IN UNEXPECTED GENEROSITY

"…remembering the words the Lord Jesus himself said: It is more blessed to give than to receive."
Acts 20:35b NIV

"You're far happier giving than getting."
The Message

Has a stranger ever paid for your coffee in the Starbucks queue? Or your toll at the bridge, or your burgers in the drive through?

We've all heard stories like this and would be thrilled if it happened to us. We'd tell everybody, we wouldn't be able to stop talking about it.

Why do we love unexpected generosity so much?

An unknown author defined generosity as "The habit of giving freely without expecting anything in return". It can involve offering time, resources or talents to aid someone in need.

In our close relationships, often without realizing it, we give to get. Not consciously, as in quid pro quo but knowing, over the long term, the giving and getting will balance out.

When we feel compelled to give unexpectedly, we are usually quiet about it. There is something reverent about meeting the needs of another, something hushed. Social psychologist Dr. Jonathan Haidt calls it elevation, a feeling we get when witnessing moral beauty, the contemplation of virtue.

Why does this kind of giving and getting touch our hearts so deeply? Why aren't we just happy and that's it?

God gives to us generously all the time. The very air we are breathing is a gift from him. If he suddenly decided to stop giving, we would all die in a matter of minutes.

What if you were the recipient of the free coffee at Starbucks and instead of being grateful, you sought out the buyer and said, "I can buy my own, thank you very much," put the coffee down and walked away?

Are we saying exactly that to God when we take for granted the unexpected generous blessings he heaps upon us every day?

God is constantly pulling from a storehouse we can't see. And since we can't see it, is it of lesser value than the free coffee?

Having an "attitude of gratitude" is a popular saying, and yes, absolutely, we need to be grateful.

But why don't we get more excited about the source of all generosity, the love that flows from God?

Do we ever think about the boundless giving that forms the very foundation of the gratitude we feel?

Unlike his children, God cannot give without loving.

We can give without loving, no problem. It's easy to write a check to a charity or ministry and feel good about ourselves for a moment.

But we cannot love without giving. The very decision to love, the very act of loving, ignites in our hearts the drive, the passion, to give.

Giving is both tangible and intangible. A gift is nice but a warm hug and a sincere, "how are you?" may mean more than a new iPad.

> *"At the end of the day, people won't remember what you said or did, they will remember how you made them feel." —Maya Angelou*

A woman in our church always has a generous, kind word for me. I don't know her very well but every time I see her, she has a something nice to say. Whenever her name is mentioned the first thing that pops into my head is: Cindy is so kind. She always makes me feel good. She lifts me up in a moment of caring and kindness and generosity.

I use the word generosity deliberately, because, you see, in her kindness there is great generosity. She is willing to set herself aside for the moment. I am sure she has bad days just like everyone, and I'm sure sometimes she doesn't feel like being nice, she is human.

Yet she makes the choice to be kind.

And in doing so, she gives me a gift, something to remember and cherish. In her unexpected generosity I find comfort. In her unexpected generosity she finds grace. And when she is kind to me, it reminds me to be kind to others, too.

Her kindness is teaching me that generosity is Christ in action through me…and through you.

Unexpected generosity is contagious. Roll around in it. Revel in it. Don't get vaccinated, catch it and pass it on!

FINDING WISDOM
IN ROMANTIC LOVE

"The Lord God said, 'It is not good for man to be alone. I will make a companion for him who corresponds to him.'" Genesis 2:18 NET

"Women were created from the rib of man to be beside him, not from his head to top him, not from his feet to be trampled by him, but from under his arm to be protected by him, near his heart to be loved by him." –Matthew Henry

One of the best-selling genres in fiction year after year is romance. We all love a love story, one that ends in a happy embrace.

The theme of these books is the idea that our loftiest goal in life is finding the right person—a soul-mate—and when we do everything in our lives will fall prettily into place. We seem to believe that romantic love is the be all and end all in life.

Why are women especially, even married ones, so drawn to

these stories? Have they turned their husbands into idols and found them wanting?

God created marriage for a number of reasons. The first obviously is for procreation. Without question the safest and most nurturing environment for kids is a stable home with a mom and dad.

God knew that children need the influence of both a mother and a father to grow up well.

Just think for a moment how different the world would be if everyone got married and remained faithfully married to the same person.

Men and women in committed marriages perpetuate and stabilize society.

Numerous studies show that 60-70% of the men currently in prison in the US were raised without a father present consistently in their lives while they were growing up.

Would our welfare rolls shrink?

Would we have less crime?

Would our kids do better in school?

A marriage with God at the center is a beautiful thing to behold. Yes, there are disagreements and at times even fights; two imperfect people cannot make a perfect relationship. But when we keep Jesus in the center of our hearts, his mighty power keeps anger and hurt from becoming destructive, and he uses conflict to draw us closer together in a better understanding of him and each other. He brings good out of bad and uses our weakness for growth. Instead of our conflicts growing, festering and pulling us apart, he uses them to help us understand our partner better and love them all the more.

Men need women to guide them. Men with Jesus in their hearts know this. I have heard men old, young and in between say, "My wife keeps me sane." "She pulls me back when I start to veer off the path God has set before me." "She brings stability into my life."

Women need men to protect them. Women with Jesus in their hearts know this. I have heard women say, "My husband makes me feel safe." "I can depend on him." "He provides for me so I can nurture him and our kids."

Interesting how God made men and women fit together for a purpose.

In Biblical marriage the man is the leader and the woman is to submit to his authority. Men are called to be servant leaders, not dictators. They are called to provide for and love their wives and even to lay down their lives for them. Stop and think about that. *Lay down their lives*. Who gets the better end of that deal?

Lack of self-esteem is a major issue with many women. We yearn to be wanted and valued as wives, mothers and lovers.

And yet so many of us find our value in being hot or sexy. We feel pressured to have sex before marriage because we know other women will if we don't, and we are programmed to think it is the only way possible to get male attention. But when we get attention this way, rather than building our sense of self-esteem, we are objectified, less than human, a plaything to be used and then discarded when the newness wears off.

God designed sex for more than just keeping the human race going. He designed it as the most special bond between a man and a woman inside the sacred union of marriage. It is the most powerful force on Earth because it can create a new life. It provides a means of expressing love between two people whose *futures are joined*.

Casual sex is demeaning and ultimately painful and destructive to both men and women alike.

During sex our brains release a hormone called oxytocin, the cuddle hormone. It causes us to bond with our partner, it stimulates feelings of love and trust. The brain is wired to view sex as a sign of intimacy and union.

So what happens to my brain when the partner it helped me to bond with leaves? When I've set myself up to get hurt yet again? Suddenly the love and trust are gone. Amputated. The brain responds the same as it would to physical pain.

There is thought currently in the scientific community that depression and anxiety in some people is linked to casual sex. It certainly is depressing to get your heart broken over and over, and it is murder to your self-esteem.

Look around the world today. Has the sexual revolution

harmed or helped us? Has it given us a stronger, more productive, more secure society?

Women love to be courted. We love engagement rings and bridal showers and weddings. Just look at the zillions of wedding-related postings on Pinterest.

I once heard a pastor say that a couple should spend less on the wedding and more on the honeymoon because that is when the marriage really begins. Good advice.

So, if romantic love is so wonderful—and it is—why doesn't it last? Why is the divorce rate so high?

For one thing, we have lost the romance of courtship. Instead of the doorbell ringing and a young man dressed up with a bouquet of flowers in his hand waiting to whisk us off to a romantic dinner in a nice restaurant, we have a booty call. Or instead of a boyfriend we have friends with benefits. Or perhaps a f buddy.

How do these kinds of relationships build-self esteem? We have been sold a big lie: casual sex is empowering, that sleeping around makes us free and strong. Really? We've been told that, "if it feels good, do it," is self evident. Is it, really? Are we living in denial of the truth that resides deeply in our hearts?

And then what happens when another period is missed and it's time to pay the piper...another broken heart, another abortion, another ruined life. How many tears are shed? Do we then feel empowered by our choices or are we awash in more guilt and shame?

Maybe we do the right thing and get married and bring a new life into a relationship that was begun with a hookup.

Sex is the most powerful force on Earth. It can create life.

Have you ever wondered why God created sex to make babies? He could have done it another way, any number of other ways.

But in his infinite wisdom he knew we needed to see a human reflection of our union with Christ. He knew we needed to bond together and stay together for the sake of our children, who are the future. And so he created sex and marriage.

As I write these words, I have been married to the most wonderful man in the world for 37 years. I am blessed to have a companion to travel alongside me as we negotiate our sojourn here on Earth.

We have stayed together and flourished because long ago we realized that love doesn't grow by gazing into each other's eyes, but by looking outward, together, in the same direction.

When we got married we made a promise that divorce wasn't an option. We used to joke murder, maybe, but not divorce.

No woman has ever been more loved and cherished than me. People tell me all the time how blessed I am to have such a wonderful husband, and it's true.

But before I knew Jesus I would look to Leonard to fill me up, to satisfy my every need and want, and I really thought he could. But he couldn't and when he didn't I would get angry and frustrated.

Do you remember the scene in *Jerry Maguire* where Tom Cruise says to Renee Zellweger, "You complete me"?

As one actor speaking to another that was a great line and made for a memorable moment on film, but no human being being can complete another. We can love, we can care for, we can support, we can even lay down our lives for those we love but we cannot make them whole.

Leonard cannot make me happy, because he is human and human love is limited. Human love changes. I don't always feel loving toward him, nor he toward me. But it doesn't matter, because the source of our love isn't human.

> *"If you try to build intimacy with another person before you've done the difficult work of getting whole, all your relationships become an attempt to complete yourself." –Dr. Les Parrott*

I remember Princess Diana saying, in the famous interview with Martin Bashir, "There were three of us in the marriage…"

There are three in mine, too. Leonard and I are both in a sold out-love affair with Jesus.

If you have made mistakes in your relationships, if you have exercised poor judgment, God is always there with an endless supply of forgiveness and mercy. He gives us another chance to begin again and again and again. He doesn't shake his finger in condemnation and judgment, he gives us the grace to start over. He gives us the ability to change. He gives us the power to become shiny and clean and *brand new*.

Begin, afresh and renewed...today.

Want more self esteem? Want to be a better wife, husband, lover? Want to be cherished and adored?

Fall in love first with the man who loved you so much he willingly died for you. He will teach you *everything* you need to know.

FINDING WISDOM
IN THE FOOD I EAT

"Eat food. Mostly plants. Not too much."
–Michael Pollan

There are plenty of arguments these days about just exactly what is the optimal diet for human beings. You have the paleo camp, the vegan group, the ovo/lacto vegetarians, the macrobiotic bunch, the nothing-heated-over-118 -degrees gang and just about every variation in between.

A few facts are beyond argument: pesticide-laden fruits and vegetables are bad. Feedlot beef and dairy products from factory farmed cows are no good. Farmed fish is a bad idea. GMOs are taking over our food supply. High fructose corn syrup makes you fat. Hydrogenated oils and trans fats will damage your heart.

All these and more, over time, are deadly.

We are hearing more and more about sustainable farming, heirloom produce, eating foods locally grown and in season and of course the ubiquitous "natural" and "organic" everything, two words so overused that they are rapidly becoming meaningless.

People used to sit down to a meal someone in the house had cooked from scratch using locally sourced ingredients. People ate because they were hungry, they needed fuel to function. I wonder sometimes how many of us have ever been truly hungry.

We are a nation of unintentional eaters. Very few of us plan what we will eat on any given day. We eat on the run. We grab something or hit the drive through and eat in the car.

How many of us experience the joy of sitting down at a well laid table with family and friends to eat a meal prepared entirely by the hands of a person we actually know? Do we ever eat slowly, savoring the flavors and textures of our God-given nourishment? Even Thanksgiving, the one day a year people actually sit down together and eat, has been hijacked by football.

Eating has changed from an enjoyable mind, body, and soul-enhancing experience to a nerve-wracking, guilt-inducing, brain-rattling ordeal. I wonder if the obesity epidemic is linked in part to the fact that we are eating more and more and enjoying it less and less. Would some of us be able to lose the excess weight that is making us so miserable if we simply learned how to recapture the lost art of dining—eating real food slowly in an atmosphere of calm and peace and beauty?

The section on food is the longest in the book, because what we put into our mouths governs so much of the rest of our lives: our energy, our attitude, our drive, our ambition. It is hard to get off the sofa when you feel like crap.

I've divided this part into bite-sized (sorry, couldn't help myself) pieces for easy assimilation and digestion. It is served to you on pretty china with flickering candles and beautiful flowers. It is hot, fragrant, delicious and very, very good for you.

Bon appetit!

FINDING WISDOM
IN THE STAFF OF LIFE

"For the Lord your God is bringing you into a good land…a land with wheat and barley."
Deuteronomy 8: 7a-8a NIV

I grew up in the middle part of the twentieth century. In the 1950s the average American woman had a 25-inch waist. She was, on average 5'3" and weighed about 125 pounds. Nowadays she is 5'4", weighs about 150 pounds and her waist measures 35 inches.

She has gotten a little taller, quite a bit heavier and a lot bigger around the middle.

After copious research and taking into consideration different body types, I concluded it takes a weight loss of about 8 pounds to take an inch off your waist. Using this formula, if a woman in the 50s wanted to add 10 inches to her waist, she would have to gain 80 pounds.

Or put another way, if today's woman wanted a 25-inch waist

she wold have to lose 70 pounds and end up weighing 80 pounds.

Now, I will grant you this is imperfect science and everybody's body is different, but...

Have you ever seen a woman from the back and thought she was slender only to have her turn around and be obviously pregnant? We all have.

But what if she turns around and instead of a baby bump she has a protruding mass of fat where her flat tummy should be?

This phenomenon is coming to be known as carb belly or wheat belly. Scientists believe it is caused by the massive consumption of refined carbohydrates, dwarf wheat being a major culprit.

The wheat of the Bible, the staff of life, bore little resemblance to the wheat of today, what we find in our beloved pizza and pasta and bread and cakes and pies and you know all what else.

Today's dwarf wheat has been cross bred and genetically manipulated to increase the yield per acre. Although the cultivation of this wheat has helped millions of people find sustenance, the unintended consequence of the "improvement" of this vital food has been massive obesity, rising Celiac disease and other serious digestive issues, an epidemic of insulin resistance that leads to type 2 diabetes and a myriad of other health issues.

By interfering with the genetic structure of a God-given plant, albeit with the best of intentions, to solve the world's hunger problem, have we helped to create wide-spread obesity and illness?

Many people are giving up grains altogether, hence the popularity of the paleo diet. Some contend we need grains; some say we don't. If you want to go quietly insane, read the mountains of research on both sides of this issue.

Or for fun, be an anthropologist for a couple hours and visit your local mall. Hang around the places that sell cinnamon rolls and pretzels and cookies and observe the people who are buying them.

Leonard and the Einkorn

I live with a man who loves wheat. My husband is Italian and was raised on pasta and pizza. He has been an ovo/lacto vegetarian for about 35 years. He actually calls himself a cheeseatarian because he has never met a cheese he didn't like.

He is happy and healthy, fit and slim and can run circles around people half his age. Every morning, seven days a week, he makes a smoothie for his breakfast. He loads the VitaMix with organic fruit, fresh juice and soaked raw nuts and seeds. He has a small snack for lunch and then we have an early dinner. Guess what he likes? Salad with pasta or pizza or sometimes a cheese and veggie omelet.

For years I cooked whole wheat pasta and made whole

wheat pizza dough even though I was less than thrilled with the dwarf wheat—at least it was whole and unrefined. Then I discovered einkorn wheat. Einkorn is a true ancient wheat; it has never been altered in any way.

First we tried einkorn spaghetti. Now, in the past, Leonard could easily eat two huge bowls of pasta. He is very active and when dinner rolls around, he is hungry. So I cooked the amount I always do and when he finished the first bowl, he was full. From one bowl? That never happens.

Then I bought some einkorn flour and made pizza. His first reaction was, wow, this is delicious, the crust has so much flavor. And again, he ate less than usual and said he was full and satisfied.

Dwarf wheat has fewer nutrients than einkorn, is lower in protein and has more gluten. It is often milled and refined, rendering it a highly processed food. By changing the nature of the plant and then processing it, the body has great difficulty recognizing it as food and has to work very hard to digest and assimilate it, often with disastrous results.

The consumption of massive amounts of dwarf wheat along with refined sugar and other simple carbohydrates is turning us into a nation of sick, exhausted, obese, wheat-bellied people.

Maybe next time you're out to dinner, ask the waiter to skip the bread basket.

PLEASE DON'T BRING HOME THE BACON

"Eat animals that have themselves eaten well."
—Michael Pollan

Bacon, sizzling bacon. Who doesn't love the smell of bacon?

If bacon—and ham and lobster and shrimp are so delicious, then why oh why did God declare them unclean and tell us not to eat them?

God chose the Israelites to be be the people from whom the Messiah would be descended. He gave them dietary and hygiene rules to insure their good health.

> *"If you listen carefully to the Lord your God and do what it right in his eyes, if you pay attention to his commandments and keep all his decrees, I will not bring on you any of the diseases I brought on the Egyptians, for I am the Lord who heals you."*
> *Exodus 5:26 NIV*

Many people today contend that since we are no longer bound under the Law, all animals are clean and good for eating. If that is true, then why are the basic natures of the animals the same as when God declared them unclean? If he had changed his mind and wanted us to eat them, why didn't he clean them up?

A few salient facts:

Pigs will eat just about anything. They will eat garbage, feces, decaying flesh. Here's a bit of trivia: the city of Philadelphia used to pay New Jersey pig farmers to take some of the city's garbage and feed it to their pigs. This practice just stopped in 1995.

Fish that do not have fins and scales are filter feeders, most of them are scavengers. Their purpose is to eat decaying, toxic matter and filter it to clean the water.

Vultures can consume toxins, including botulism, that would kill a human and be just fine.

Rabbits, although seemingly clean, were forbidden by God to eat. Scientists now tell us rabbits re-consume part of their feces as they don't have separate stomachs to get the nutrients out of their food the way a cow does.

Is science finally catching up to God?

Could it be God created certain creatures as a clean-up crew and not for us to eat?

God had big plans for the Israelites. He planned to have the

Messiah, Jesus Christ, the savior of the world born from the lineage of David. He was going to call certain men to be disciples of Jesus during his ministry on Earth and later they would found and build the Church. He needed a strong gene pool. He didn't need a bunch of sickly, weak, people who would be too tired to spread the greatest news ever.

And so he gave them a set of guidelines to help them live healthy, happy, productive lives.

He wants the same for us. He has big plans for you and me. Who knows what he might have in mind. Will you be there when he calls? Healthy, strong and ready to go?

Remember, you are not only what you eat, you are what you eat, eats. Grass or garbage, you decide.

A MODERN DAY
SCHOOL FIELD TRIP

When I was a kid in elementary school, once a year we got to go on a field trip. I remember visiting the local newspaper and watching through a huge window as gigantic rolls of paper ran through the press and churned out the news. We visited a pasta factory and saw tubes of macaroni being extruded, cut and dried for our favorite mac and cheese. Once we went to a bakery, where they gave us chocolate chip cookies. I liked that one a lot.

One time another class got to go to a local family farm. The best part, I was told, was watching the cows getting milked. The farmer even offered the kids a taste; I don't know if anyone tried it.

Fast forward 40 years.

Teacher: "Who wants to go on a field trip?"

Kids: (waving their hands) "I do, I do!"

Teacher: "Okay, who likes hamburgers?"

Thirty hands go up.

Teacher: "Do you know where hamburgers come from?"

Kids: "Cows!"

Teacher: "That's right. And where do cows live?"

Kids: "On farms."

Teacher: "Right again. Today we are going to visit a farm where you will learn about animal husbandry, which means learning about how animals are raised. The cows we will see today are being grown for food, the hamburgers you all like. So are you ready?"

Kids: "Yay!"

As the school bus gets closer to the farm, the kids are talking excitedly. "Have you ever seen a real cow?" "What do cows eat?" "Cows are really big!" "Hey, did you fart?" "No way!"

"Miss Teacher, something stinks!"

The teacher smiles, "Oh that's just the cows. We'll be at the farm in a minute."

The bus turns off the highway and the kids stare out, not at a grassy pasture dotted with cows placidly eating grass and flicking away flies with their tails, but hundreds, maybe thousands of cows, all crammed together tightly in metal pens with no grass in sight.

The children reluctantly climb off the bus holding their noses. One little girl hides behind the teacher; the other kids stare, wide eyed, at the scene before them.

Finally one kid ventures, "Is this really a farm?"

"Yes," says the teacher, "this is a factory farm."

This field trip will never take place. The sight of a filthy, stinking feedlot is far too disturbing to ever inflict on a tender child. But every time that child eats a fast food burger, he is keeping the factory farms in business.

Factory farms exist to satisfy the voracious market for abundant cheap meat. We abuse animals and pervert their natural instincts so we can have meat and more meat, as much as we want, anytime we want it and for very little money. The animals are fattened up with artificial hormones so they can be slaughtered sooner, in 11-14 months instead of 4-5 years and pumped full of antibiotics for the many diseases they contract while jammed in a pen, where they spend their days in misery and pain.

A day in the life of a pastured cow would look something like this: Mosey around in open pasture, chew on some grass, spit it up and chew some more, ruminate away until milking time. Relax while your udder is being emptied, have a nice sleep (in the barn if it's cold outside). Repeat. Along the way you will have a calf or two or ten. Finally it will be time to give your life to feed humans. You will have been well treated and lived your life the way God intended. Your meat will provide high-quality nourishment, protein, vitamins and minerals. You will have fulfilled your purpose.

Your counterpart at the factory farm isn't having such a good time. Instead of grass to chew, corn is dumped into a bin for you and a hundred of your pen-mates to eat. You swallow the corn and in a few minutes one of your tummies starts to rumble. You feel your skin stretching as gas builds up with no means of escape. Eating grass would cause you to burp and feel much better, but alas, with corn that doesn't happen. Now you are having trouble breathing because your bloated belly is pressing against your heart and lungs. Pretty soon one of your caretakers sees you are in distress. He drags you off to the "hospital", where he roughly shoves a hose down your throat, which is supposed to allow the trapped grass to escape. It that doesn't work, he has other ideas, like slicing open your tummy.

Okay. Enough. Are you saying I should give up meat and become a vegetarian?

Not necessarily. What I am saying is do we really need so much cheap meat? Could we eat less and eat better? Yes, grass fed beef is more expensive. It is also far, far healthier. Would you prefer a burger or steak from a clean, grass-fed cow or a drug-filled one from a factory farm? Ethics aside, which one do you want to eat? Which one do you want to give your kids?

Instead of meat at every dinner, how about beef say, two or three times a week? The other four to five nights, maybe chicken (pastured please, the chickens don't like being mistreated, either). Or how about a big baked potato with butter and cheese? Or einkorn or quinoa pasta with a rich tomato sauce and a nice salad? Wild-caught salmon is always good. How about breakfast for dinner, maybe eggs and home fries. Yum! When you do have meat, have four or six ounces instead of eight, and surround it with lots of buttered vegetables. If you're grilling, grill the veggies, too.

Treat meat like the special gift it is. Enjoy it. Savor it.

Once you get used to the best, it will be easy to skip the drive through.

And the cows will thank you.

FINDING WISDOM
IN THE JUNK FOOD I USED TO
EAT

"To be normal, to drink Coca Cola and eat Kentucky Fried Chicken, is to be in a conspiracy against yourself." –Jerry Fletcher

"Bacon-wrapped Oreos. God bless America." –Jim Gaffigan

As followers of Christ we live by the Great Commandment and the Great Commission. We love God, we love others and we spread the Good News by word and deed. We have a longing in our hearts to build the kingdom.

Sadly, we can do none of this if we are sick, exhausted and barely making it through the day. How can we "go and make disciples of all nations" if we can't get off the sofa?

God designed our bodies to require food and movement. He provided certain kinds of plants and animals to keep us nourished and in good shape for our assignments here on earth.

Have you ever heard anyone say:

My goal is to be obese?

My goal is to have a disease?

My goal is to be dependent on prescription drugs?

Or I want all of the above for my kids?

Of course not. And yet many of us are all these things: fat, sick and looking for a drug to fix us.

Everywhere processed food goes, disease follows. Refined sugar, modern dwarf wheat, hydrogenated oils, high fructose corn syrup, artificial flavors and colors, pesticide residues and more are found in every aisle of the grocery store.

Worst of all, processed food is aggressively marketed to children. Kids are naturally attracted to bright colors, funny images and happy sounds. Build brand loyalty with a child and you have a customer for life. Marketers are well aware of this. Add a clown and free plastic toys and the kids are hooked. Hooked means addicted, physically and mentally dependent on a substance or activity. No more choices, just repetitive, destructive behavior.

Is this the life you want for your child? For yourself?

The fruit of the spirit we all like least is the last one: self-control. The others, love–joy–peace–patience–kindness–goodness–faithfulness and gentleness sound lovely and sweet, like poetry.

But then at the end comes self-control.

So I am joyful and patient and kind and feeling pretty good about myself and wham! You are telling me that God wants me to put the brakes on myself? Yes. God wants us to make the kind of choices that will move us forward, not back.

But I like that donut; I want that donut.

Of course you do. So do I. Besides, what's wrong with one little donut? Churches have been serving them in their fellowship halls for decades. How bad can they be? Why am I picking on the lowly little donut?

Donuts are one of the most destructive "foods" you can put into your mouth. In just one bite you have the unholy trinity of trans fat, sugar and dwarf wheat. Depending on the kind of donut you choose, you can add in a whole host of other stuff, artificial, fake, this and that.

The donut is a seemingly innocuous little treat that, over time, will weaken and eventually destroy the temple of the Holy Spirit…your body.

Can you relate to the following story?

Sam and the Donut

Sam really like donuts, but he knows they harm God's temple so he made a plan to eat only one donut on Sunday morning at church and that's it, just one a week. Sometimes he thinks about donuts, and not on Sunday mornings, but his willpower is strong and so far he hasn't given in.

This particular Wednesday Sam is going to an important meeting. There will be a speaker there Sam has been dying to hear. He is very excited.

The moment he walks into the room he sees, right next to the coffee, a platter of donuts. There on top is his favorite, the one he gets every Sunday. Immediately he wants that maple bar. He can practically smell it. An intense craving takes ahold of him. He wants it. Now.

So what will happen next? Will Sam keep his commitment to himself and God and say no to the donut? Will he just have half and throw the rest away? Will he cave and eat the whole thing?

Sam ate a donut three days ago, so the experience is still fresh and vivid in his mind. Even if Sam turns away and doesn't eat the donut, his concentration is ruined. His focus has shifted away from the meeting he was looking forward to, and his energy is being consumed fighting the craving.

Instead of experiencing the morning through a big, roomy lens, he now sees it though the hole in the donut.

Can Sam take or leave his treat, or is he in thrall to it?

Has his once-a-week donut habit become an addiction?

If addiction is a "persistent compulsive dependence on a behavior or substance"and compulsive means "an irresistible urge especially one that is against one's conscious wishes," is Sam addicted to donuts?

Sam could be me. Sam could be you.

So how do we have our cake and eat it without turning into junk food junkies?

We can save treats for special occasions, birthdays, Christmas and the like. Remember, the planning and anticipation of a goodie is half the fun. When we do indulge, we can make the sweet ourselves, that way we can control the ingredients. Or buy the treat from a store that is interested in nutrition as well as profits. Real butter beats fake fat any day.

A small serving of homemade butterscotch pudding with homemade whipped cream eaten slowly and savored once in awhile is so much more fun and enjoyable than chowing down a candy bar every afternoon in three ravenous bites.

We can raise our kids on real food and help them to develop a palate that craves the delicious flavors and textures that come from God, not from a laboratory or factory. We can help spare them from a lifetime of cravings and so, unlike Sam, they can be focused and excited about the work God is calling them to.

And your kids will teach their kids to eat well. And on and on through the future. What a wonderful legacy to leave for the next generation.

A PRAYER IN GRATITUDE FOR A FRUIT SMOOTHIE

Dear Heavenly Father,

Thank you for this berry smoothie I am about to eat. Thank you for creating strawberries and raspberries and blueberries. Thank you for carefully weaving them into perfect little containers of goodness. Thank you for the phytochemicals that give them their bright colors and for the loads of antioxidants they contain that protect against disease and help strengthen my immune system. Thank you for their high water content that hydrates my skin and keeps my waistline slim and for the fiber the keeps my digestive system working well and the folate that helps maintain my healthy blood pressure. Thank you for all the vitamins and minerals they contain—I can't even remember all of them! And thank you for the banana that makes my drink so thick and smooth and delicious.

And Lord, I thank you that, in your infinite wisdom,

you created the perfect foods to keep me healthy and humming along so my days may be spent serving you with energy and joy. I ask you to bless this smoothie to the nourishment of my body.

I pray all this in Jesus' name,

Amen

FINDING WISDOM
IN MOVING MY BODY

"For the Lord sees not as a man does; for man looks at the outward appearance but the Lord looks at the heart." 1 Samuel 16:7b NLT

On a Treadmill to Nowhere

I used to truly hate exercise. I still hate sweating. I hate gyms. My husband is a retired personal fitness trainer and has worked out all his life. People used to ask me what kind of workout I did and I would say, are you serious?

But one day I started thinking about the miracle of the human body, mine in particular. I looked at my legs and thought about how God designed them to carry me anywhere he wants me to go, how my hands allow me to do the cooking I love, even at this moment how they are allowing me to write these words.

I began to realize, as the psalmist said, I am so fearfully and wonderfully made. I thought about the zillion little things we do every day without thinking because of the miracle of movement.

I still hate organized exercise. I hate lifting weights. I hate treadmills. I don't get the point of taking step after step in the same place, boring beyond belief! If you're going to walk go outside for goodness sake! I will never get it.

But when I thought about how acknowledging the miracle of my body and the one who created it was worship, it changed my attitude. When I move in thanks to God, I am showing him my love.

I now understand that exercise is not about how I look, about fitting into size ___ jeans. It is not about being cut or bulky. It's not about how far I can run or how fast. It's not a competition. It's not even about how much better I feel when I move—that's just a fringe benefit.

Exercise is an attitude of worship and gratitude to God for giving me the ability to move.

> *"I believe God made me for a purpose but he also made me fast. When I run, I feel his pleasure."*
> *–Eric Liddell*

Now when I get ready to exercise, I thank God that I *can* walk. I thank him for the miracle of my body. I thank him for the iPod that allows me to listen to audiobooks or the beautiful sound of praise music as I walk. I thank him for the great privilege of being able to put one foot in front of the other. I thank him for the trees and the fresh air and the birdsong. I now exercise in a posture of gratitude.

Move your hand right now. How does it work? Study it. Think about the majesty of a being who is able to design such a useful tool. Speak your thanks, don't hold back. Think often about the miracle that is *your* body. Use it, move it for the glory of your creator. What a gift it is!

My shoes are tied, see you later!

> *If you think too much, walk. If you can't think, walk. If you think poorly, walk some more.*
> *—Pierre-Robert Hélaine*

FINDING WISDOM
IN REST

*"You and your family are to remember the Sabbath
Day; set it apart and keep it holy. You have six days to
do all your work but the seventh day is to be
different." Exodus 20: 8-10a The Voice*

Vacation, oh boy I'm going on vacation! Counting the days,
can't wait to go!

Is it the weekend yet?

TGIF!

Everybody loves a break from routine, a time out of our
normal routine to rest, to relax, to have fun, to do something
different...or to do nothing at all.

God clearly understood the need for rest when he
commanded, not suggested, that we take one day off a
week. He modeled a life of work and accomplishment
during the six days of creation, and on the seventh day he

rested. God wasn't tired, he just wanted us to see the importance of rest.

Everybody knows what it feels like to be tired. Chronic fatigue leads to a whole host of problems, including illness. For many of us, rest and sleep have become luxuries instead of the vital necessities they truly are.

A Sabbath day is more than just physical rest. It is a time to calm our hearts and minds in the reminder of the blessed assurance of salvation through our Lord, Jesus Christ. It is a time to pause in a moment of gratitude for all he has done, is doing and will do for us.

Here is his reminder:

> *"Are you tired? Worn out? Burned out on religion? Come to me. Get away with me and you'll recover your life. I'll show you how to take a real rest. Walk with me and work with me—watch how I do it. Learn the unforced rhythms of grace. I won't lay anything heavy or ill-fitting on you. Keep company with me and you'll learn how to live freely and lightly."*
> *Matthew 11:28-29 The Message*

Unforced rhythms…isn't that great?

Imagine what your life would be like if, one day a week, every week, you simply hit the off switch. What would your week look like?

How would you feel if you knew, at the beginning of every week, you would have a true day off.? Every six days a real break?

Pastor John Ortberg once asked Christian philosopher Dallas Willard for spiritual direction. He had just moved to a new, fast-paced church with his wife and two young children. He was feeling overwhelmed and in need of guidance. Willard's advice was short and succinct: "You must ruthlessly eliminate hurry from your life."

Busyness, overcommitment, rushing, scrambling to get everything done kills our innate ability to tap into the inner wisdom God has provided. We cannot hear his still, small voice when we are always preoccupied and in a hurry.

> "Be **still** and know that I am God."
> Psalm 46:10a NLT (emphasis mine)

So, what would a Sabbath look like? It wouldn't look the same for everyone, but it would be a time to turn away from all the musts and shoulds and oughts and embrace the goodness of God's grace in rest. A good place to start is church. Worship and get filled with the word of God. Take a walk in nature and enjoy the beauty of all God has created. Play a board game with your kids. Eat your favorite food. Lump out and let the rest of the world roll on by. It will still be there tomorrow.

Leonard and I take Sundays off. We go to church, we take walks, we play games, sometimes we watch a movie, but mostly we simply enjoy the change from our everyday lives and relax knowing that by obeying God's law on rest, he will maximize the other six days and allow us to accomplish everything he has set before us to do. We trust that his prescribed rest will allow the remaining time to be maximized for his glory.

And it always is. *God is able to do something we can't…he can stretch time. When we follow his plan, he will see to it that everything he wants to be accomplished is.*

When I set up a schedule for the writing of this book, I continued to take a day of rest. Sometimes God would put an idea in my head about something he wanted said in these pages, and I would go and write it down and then close the notebook firmly and put it away until Monday. I learned that God gives me ideas any time he chooses, but he blesses those ideas when I use them in his way and in his time.

So why not use your God-given day of rest to step out of your daily life and and enjoy all your creator has given you? Remind yourself of his priceless gift of salvation. Go and hear the word of God being preached. Worship him in song. Remind yourself that everything, *everything,* you have is a gift from him. Pause and reflect on just how much you are loved. Set aside thoughts of the rest of the week and revel in the goodness of all you are as a beloved child of God. Honor him.

And then just…*ahhhhhh relax.*

FINDING WISDOM
IN MY HOME

"By wisdom a house is built and through understanding it is established; through knowledge its rooms are filled with rare and beautiful treasures."
Proverbs 24:3-4 NIV

When someone asks, "where do you live?", what do you answer? Probably with the name of your town or street. But think about the question. Where do you *live*?

Actually, you live in every space you inhabit, anywhere your body is residing at any given moment. You live at work, at the grocery store, at church. You live at the soccer game and the dance recital and everywhere else.

But there is something different about your dwelling, the place you call home. It's more than just a place where you sleep and eat and wash your clothes. It is even more than the place you hang out with your friends and family.

In *The Odyssey*, Homer is desperate to get back home.

Ikea has built a massive, worldwide business on one idea: home is the most important place in the world.

We all know how great it is to travel, but it's oh so lovely to return home...I just can't wait to sleep in my own bed!

Is it the comfort, the familiarity, that makes home so appealing? Is it the sense of safety from an often scary, threatening world?

It is all of this and more.

Your home is your sanctuary. Whether you own or rent, the walls belong to you. Why not make it a true place of rest and healing, clutter free and serene?

What if your kitchen was full of good, nourishing food that doesn't come in boxes or cans? What if your cleaning products weren't full of nasty chemicals? Ditch the dryer sheets and, if you can, hang your clothes outside to dry in the sun.

What if your home was filled with greenery, plants and flowers? What if your walls were painted soft, soothing colors? What if you had dinner on nice dishes, maybe with candles glowing, and the TV and phones turned off and music playing?

This is what home is all about: a refuge from the noisy, frantic world that lurks outside your door.

I remember reading a long time ago about when Martha Stewart was negotiating her first contract with Kmart. As she was describing the kinds of products she wanted in her signature line, the CEO said to her, "But Martha, Kmart shoppers don't live like that." I will never forget her answer. She smiled at him and said, "But they *want* to."

She knew very well we all want a home that expresses who we are. We want order and comfort and beauty in our dwellings.

My friend Linda does something every day I think is brilliant. When she finishes her evening meal, she cleans up and then sets her breakfast tray for the next morning. She puts her cup and plate on a tray with silverware and a nice napkin. She tells me that in the morning she feels greeted and special, as though she were in a lovely hotel. She starts her day with tea and toast (she is British) and a bit of the Bible. She feels set on course for whatever the day will bring. The two-minute act of preparing for the next day pays off in huge dividends every time.

One way to create a warm, welcoming home is to purge. Get rid of all the clutter and mess. It is hard to feel peaceful in a pile of rubble.

Another way is to establish a simple cleaning routine. Enlist the help of your entire family. If a kid can use a cell phone, he can operate a washer.

Finally, begin to view your home as the precious gift from God it truly is. Thank him for the roof over your head and for protection from the elements. When you do household chores, thank him that the dishes you are washing were filled with food that gave you nourishment and pleasure. As you scrub the toilet, thank him for your bathroom, that you have hot water and soap and shampoo.

When you tuck your kids into bed, thank him that they are warm and safe and don't have to worry about where they will be living tomorrow.

One day all followers of Christ will live together in heaven. Jesus used the word "mansion" in John 14:2-3 to describe our heavenly home. The word *mone*, in Greek, means abode, the act of staying or residing. He is preparing for us a place to live. Why not treat our earthly homes as practice for our heavenly homes?

Fill them with serenity and beauty.

And remember, whenever you see an empty chair, it isn't really empty at all. It is occupied by a man with scars on his hands and feet and side wearing gleaming robes of the purest white keeping diligent watch over you and all the members of your household.

What a privilege to keep our homes clean and beautiful and prepared for *him*.

FINDING WISDOM WITH MY STUFF: THE RICHES OF LESS

"Steep your life in God reality, God initiative, God provisions. Don't worry about missing out. You'll find all your everyday human concerns will be met."
Matthew 6:33 The Message

"The learned man aims for more. But the wise man decreases. And then decreases again."
–James Altucher

"Treat yourself to a little retail therapy."

"Whoever said laughter is the best medicine obviously never tried shopping."

"I was sad but then I bought something. Now I feel better."

"Keep calm and go shopping."

"Whoever said money doesn't buy happiness doesn't know where to shop."

What do all these quotes have in common? Are they funny? Not really. They are all about sadness or anxiety or depression. The smell of quiet desperation in a shopping mall is stronger than the Cinnabons.

We all know things don't make us happy. Look at how the minimalism movement is gaining ground. Just Google "tiny house" or "living with less."

And yet we buy and buy and then buy some more.

And then store and maintain and clean and insure. And finally get rid of to make room for more.

Oh, yes, and pay the bill. Many of us are in debt to all our stuff.

Some of us want the latest techno gadget. Maybe a shiny new car. Perhaps we like initials or logos on our clothes. Did you know most fashion designers don't themselves wear what they sell? Until they send you a check, do you really want to be a free walking billboard?

Will I truly be more creative if I buy a luxury car? The ad says I will.

If I wear a certain perfume will I have a gorgeous husband and kids and frolic all day on the beach? Really?

Or worse, if I feed my preschooler fast food with plastic toys and a clown, will he be happy all day long?

The average American home now has more televisions than people: 2.73 sets vs 2.55 people. Many people leave their TVs on the entire time they are home and awake. What do you think happens when we are constantly bombarded with advertising?

I am personally vulnerable to the almighty Apple. My house is full of MacBooks and iPhones and iPads. I love them because they do what they are supposed to and serve me well, at least until new technology renders them obsolete.

I need my computer and my phone. But do I need another trinket from China? Am I using shopping to fill a void that never stays filled?

What if I bought better and bought less? What if I satisfied my need for something new by buying things that will nurture me and the people around me?

What if I bought a big bunch of flowers and put them on my desk at work for everyone to enjoy?

What if I bought a really nice bottle of wine and then cooked a beautiful meal to go with it and shared it with my family or friends?

What if, instead of buying my child another toy, I got them a membership to a children's museum or zoo and then made dates to take them and spend the day together?

What if we stopped buying things we can't afford and don't need, to impress people we don't even like, and started spending our money on experiences to share with the people we love? And what if, regularly, not just at Christmas, we gave money and time to help people in need?

Things are static; they don't change. That is why we tire of them. They become boring, and the thrill dies. But experiences live on, they grow, and they turn into lasting memories.

> *"Experiences tend to be associated with deeper personal meaning than possessions."*
> *—Social Psychologist Leaf Van Boven*

As we get older, won't it be lovely to look back and remember the vacations, the dinners, the ski trips, the football games, the concerts, all the things we shared with others? We will think about the funny things that happened, the bonds that were forged, the people we still hold close.

It will be amazing how much our lives were enriched every time we skipped that trip to the mall and indulged in a different kind of therapy.

FINDING WISDOM
IN PRAYER

"Jesus often withdrew to lonely places and prayed."
Luke 5:16 NIV

"Prayer is talking with God about what we are doing together." –Dallas Willard

I have never met anyone who is satisfied with their prayer life. We worry we aren't praying enough or we're saying the wrong words or even, if we are doing it right, God isn't hearing us and on and on…

Even those of us who have developed the habit of a quiet time every day with God still aren't content with our communication skills when it comes to our creator. We don't have any problem talking with our family or friends, so why do we stress out when it comes to talking with our heavenly father?

The easy answer is, well, I can't see him and he doesn't answer back, so how do I know I'm getting through? Or I have been asking for _____ for a long time and nothing is happening—so I must be doing something wrong. Or so and so prays eloquently and I stumble and mumble, God must be bored with me!

Or maybe I think God is so awesome and powerful, does he really have time for me?

Think back to when you first fell in love or when you started to get to know your best friend. Think about how you felt at the beginning of the significant relationships in your life.

When we are first attracted to someone, romantically or as a friend, we are very interested in everything they have to say. We want to know more about them, their experiences, their opinions, everything. We want to share ourselves in the same way. As the relationship deepens and grows, we begin to share our hopes and dreams, our pain and disappointments. After a while we may not talk as much because we have established a comfortable, safe place where we can just be together. But we know our beloved friend loves us, cares deeply and will support us when we need them.

But even the best of friends, the most loving spouse, the closest brother or sister is not always able to be be there one hundred percent of the time. No matter how much we love and care for another, we are limited by our human nature. Even the most loving of us gets bored and exasperated hearing the same hurt, the same problem, even the same joke repeated again and again.

This is where God is very different. He never gets bored with us. We may get tired of ourselves, but he doesn't. He cares deeply about every single aspect of our lives. He is with us all the time. He knows our every thought, our every feeling.

Sometimes we think we have to tune into God like an old-time radio before we go to him in prayer. If we don't stop first and get his attention, we think he isn't really noticing us. We may think we have to raise our hands like a kid in school to get him to see us.

Not so. He is tuned into us all the time; we just aren't abiding in him.

Abide is a wonderful word we don't use much anymore. Abide means to continue, to endure, to remain. Not necessarily to do anything but, as we do in our closest relationships, simply to *be*.

When we abide in Jesus, we are resting in the knowledge that he is with us. Whether we are consciously thinking about him at any given moment or not doesn't matter—he is with us. He doesn't snap to attention when we call on him; he is there, quietly, patiently, attentive and waiting...always.

We think of our lives in terms of seasons. We have a season of childhood, a season of schooling, a season of work, of marriage, of raising a family and finally a time of retirement.

People come and go throughout the seasons. Some are there for a brief time, some stay longer, but eventually they will all leave. One day we will be reunited with God's children in heaven but in the meantime we have only one true lasting relationship, and that is with our creator.

Sometimes we have long conversations with our loved ones. Sometimes we just send a brief email or text message.

God likes both. He loves communication in any form; he just wants to hear from us. He is interested in everything we do. He loves to be praised and thanked for all he does. He likes to hear what we have learned. He is interested in our quandaries, our struggles, and he never tires of hearing about our problems, our pain, our fears, whether we are happy, sad or in between.

Sometimes we struggle with words, we think we have to perfectly articulate our thoughts and feelings or God doesn't understand. Not true.

If we just sit quietly and let our feelings cascade over minds and hearts, God will understand immediately exactly what we are trying to say. We just have to open up and let him in.

He knows our hearts perfectly, so he reads between the lines and understands us in a way no human being will ever be able to. He is endlessly patient and never, ever condemns us, belittles us, puts us down or thinks any less of us no matter what we do or say.

In his infinite kindness and love, he convicts our hearts, draws us into repentance and as we humbly confess, he forgives us immediately and sends us out to thrive and grow.

Now seriously, why wouldn't we want to talk to him? All the time? We complicate prayer; God doesn't. He just wants to hear from us so we can stay close to him.

Close your eyes right now and send him a mental text message. You will make his day.

> *"Our sense of relief doesn't come from God's answers as much as from God's attention." –David Whitehead*

FINDING WISDOM
IN MUSIC

"Serve the Lord with gladness, come before his presence with singing." Psalm 100:2 NLT

"Everlasting, your light will shine when all else fails, never ending your glory goes beyond all fame. And the cry of my heart is to bring you praise from the inside out, Lord my soul cries out."

(From The Inside Out
Music and Lyrics by Joel Houston)

The Wisdom of Worship

There are a multitude of ways to worship God. Any time we acknowledge his power and strength and love we are worshipping him. When we remember the price Jesus paid for our salvation, we are worshipping. When we come before the Lord in gratitude, that is worship. Most of us strive to lead a worshipful lifestyle.

But when we hear the word worship, what do we think of first? Music of course.

Did you know music is mentioned in at least 44 books of the Bible? Jesus himself sang a hymn at the last supper.

Music has the ability to touch our hearts in a wholly unique and meaningful way. God created music for us to enjoy and gave us the ability to arrange it in hundreds of different styles and genres.

Music helps us to de-stress, to focus. It takes us inward, away from the unrelenting distractions that can keep us from sensing God's presence.

When we worship God in song, it is one way of aligning ourselves with him.

When we praise him in song, we are lifted up, our hearts are lightened, our faith is brought to the forefront and made stronger. Heartfelt praise and worship, especially through music, opens our sometimes stony hearts to feel God's love.

When we sing to God we acknowledge his strength, power and love over our lives. We look up, sometimes lifting our hands toward the heavens as we give ourselves over to our creator and accept the love that pours down into our hearts.

When we sing in groups, it brings us closer to God and each other.

When we listen or sing alone, it reminds us of the personal relationship we all have with God and how he has infinite time and attention for each of us, every moment of every day.

The more we praise God for who he is, the more we raise ourselves up to him in trust and faith and obedience, the more we feel his Holy Spirit in our hearts.

Singing to God, singing about God, reminds us of his character and our connection, that we have direct access and communication 24/7. He is always there, he is never too busy to give us his full attention.

Sometimes we sing out of pure joy. We praise God for the peace and happiness that fills our hearts.

At other, painful times, we may not have the words to pray. Grief and pain and struggles of all kinds can render us inarticulate and make God seem far away.

The very act of listening to God being worshipped, being praised in song and tearfully stumbling over the words as we try to sing along, reminds us in a powerful way that God is, in fact, not far away at all but right here, right now.

In our darkest moments of despair, God hears our wordless groans and gives us, through music, the words we cannot find.

We are wired to worship—God made us that way. If we don't worship him, we will worship *something*. And if it isn't God, it will be something that won't last, something that can be taken away, something we can lose.

Why not worship the only One who will never leave you, who will never let you down, *whose love you cannot lose no matter what.*

Why not worship your creator who forgave your sins, wiped them out completely. Then gave you a reason and a purpose for living and finally, one day, a home in heaven where you will dwell with him forever in unshakable peace and harmony.

Ponder that for a moment.

Then find the wisdom of worship through the gift of music.

Why not sing to him right now?

FINDING WISDOM
IN THE CULTURE OF
CELEBRITY WORSHIP

*"Will the doctor with the cure for cancer please sit
down! Here comes Marla Maples!"*
Dennis Miller, The Rants

Some of you may be thinking, who is Marla Maples? She was
popular a while back; her heyday was in the 1990s. As I
recall, she really didn't do much except marry and divorce a
billionaire, and then after a few years we lost interest in her
and she has since been replaced by a parade of those
famous for being famous celebrities.

As I write this a certain dark haired mother and her three
daughters reign, the most popular of the daughters is known
for her generous backside. Years from now readers of this
book may not know who I'm talking about, but today most of
us do.

There have been volumes written on celebrity culture, on
why, exactly, we are so fascinated with what is going on in

the lives of people we don't know. Why does it matter what they are doing or who they're doing it with, what they're wearing or where they're going?

Most of us have a favorite musician or film or sports star we especially like and admire, and it's fun to keep track of what they're up to. That's okay, as long as we enjoy them for what they are and don't elevate them to a place of idolatry. There is nothing wrong with admiring and enjoying the talent of another person.

But what happens when we are irresistibly drawn to people who do nothing but preen in front of the camera, spend massive amounts of money on parties and events to glorify themselves and constantly parade before the public in an insatiable bid for attention? What exactly is there to celebrate abut the way they live?

Why are we so attracted to these people, especially when the celebrity landscape is littered with the results of this pointless, over-the-top way of life? Suicide, drug overdoses, alcoholism, domestic violence—the price paid is a heavy one. By some estimates the divorce rate in Hollywood is 80%.

As we gaze into the VIP room at the latest hot club knowing we will never be invited in, how does that make us feel? The word envy come to mind. Does anyone enjoy feeling envious? So why do we do it?

I had the interesting experience of visiting Studio 54 in New York City during the short time it was the hottest nightclub on Earth. I was able to get past the velvet rope because it was a weeknight and I was with someone who knew the gatekeeper.

There was a rumor swirling around that a certain very famous actress/singer was planning to stop by that evening.

I looked around at people as they pretended they weren't watching the door, hoping, *hoping* she would arrive and they would get a glimpse of her superstar aura close up.

Finally she did show up. She's here, she's here! But on closer inspection it wasn't her after all, it was a man dressed up to look like her, a drag queen.

The dance floor cleared to make way for her. She took the center, resplendent in a sparkly silver gown, hair and makeup done exactly as her namesake, and proceeded to dance surrounded by a crown of admirers. For a few hours he was a celebrity, famous and admired. In his own jeans and a shirt, left behind in some tiny Brooklyn or Queens apartment or somewhere else on the big impersonal island of Manhattan, he might not have made it past the velvet rope. But looking like a fabulous diva he was welcomed and, for a brief, shining moment, he was a *star*.

I will never forget that night. I was quite young at the time, and it has taken me years of reflection and observation of our pervasive celebrity culture to begin to look critically at what it says about the celebrities themselves and the people who worship them. What exactly are we doing when we buy another gossip magazine or turn on an infotainment show? And what drives a person to long to be on the cover of those magazines or to be the headliner on those shows?

An insatiable ego, a constant need for attention and admiration that is never, ever fulfilled. The more they get, the more they want. And there's something else.

In *How Evil Works,* David Kupelian proposes an interesting idea: we know that worship is meant for God alone, and when human beings are elevated to a place of worship, as celebrities often are, the very act of being worshipped does strange things to them. Since our God is a jealous God who commands us to put nothing before him, when we constantly crave admiration and attention we are entering into some very dangerous territory.

Have you ever been praised excessively? Did it make you feel uncomfortable? I have and it did. I wanted to say, okay, thank you and let's move on. I cannot possibly remain balanced on your pedestal.

I clearly know my limitations, and if I ignore the reality of my shortcomings, pride will start to replace the healthy self-esteem that resides in my heart because I have found my true identity in Christ. When I am praised too much, I begin to feel impatience and contempt for the person fawning over me. I once heard a celebrity tell a fan who was falling all over them to "Get a life."

The more I allow myself to be elevated by excessive praise, the more blind I become to the reality of who I am. If I get elevated to the level of celebrity, I can surround myself all day long with people who are constantly telling me how wonderful I am. The more they praise me, the more I will come to despise them.

Then I will have to find someone else to serve me, and the cycle will start all over. I will have a hard time telling whether someone likes me for me or for what I can do for them. I will grow a massive sense of entitlement and an ego that will take on a life of its own. Oh, and the first time I take a misstep, the press and public will turn on me like a mad dog. It is no small wonder so many celebrities who "have it all" crash and burn.

Think about it, would you like to live that way?

As a follower of Christ, every time I participate in celebrity worship, every time I spend my time or money on furthering the cause, I am making the road to that person's destruction all that much easier and smoother.

Do I want to participate in destroying someone's life? Jesus tells us to love others as ourselves. That means I must love you too much to participate in your demise.

Put the fan magazine back. Turn off the TV. Think of a celebrity who is in real trouble and pray for them. They need your prayers far more than your adoration.

FINDING WISDOM
IN COMMON INCOMPLETE
QUOTES

"The truth shall set you free."
—Found on Buildings at Numerous Colleges and
Other Institutions

Jesus said to the people who believed in him, "You
are truly my disciples if you remain faithful to my
teachings. And you will know the truth and the truth
will set you free." John 8: 31-32 NLT

I was at a conference recently and the speaker flashed the
Serenity Prayer up on the big screen. It has been attributed
to Reinhold Niebuhr (1892-1971), a theologian, pastor,
professor and author of numerous writings on politics,
religion and history. The prayer on the screen was longer
than the one most of us are familiar with. We know it as:

"God grant me the serenity to accept what cannot be
changed, the courage to change what can be and the
wisdom to know the difference."

There is more than one version of this prayer, Niebuhr himself said it may have been floating around for years, but he took credit for this, the final form:

> *"God give me the grace to accept with serenity the things that cannot be changed*
> *Courage to change the things which should be changed*
> *And the wisdom to distinguish the one from the other*
> *Living one day at a time*
> *Accepting hardship as a pathway to peace*
> *Taking as Jesus did this sinful world as it is*
> *Not as I would have it*
> *Trusting that You will make all things right*
> *If I surrender to your will*
> *So that I may be reasonably happy in this life*
> *And supremely happy with You forever in the next*
> *Amen"*

Look at the differences in the short and long versions of this prayer and in John 8:31-32. What happened to the parts about "if I surrender to your will" and "remaining faithful to my teachings"?

Today we live in a culture that tells us all truth is relative—what is true for you may not be true for me.

The problem with this idea is that we all demand truth in every area of our lives.

Nobody wants to be lied to by a spouse or a friend...by anyone.

We expect the courts to convict the guilty.

We expect our news reports to be truthful.

When we fly, we want to be assured by the airline company that the pilot has completed the proper training and is fit and experienced to fly the plane. The truth is I don't want an inebriated person flying the plane, and neither do you.

Truth is simply the way things are. We can believe the Earth is flat, but that does not make it so. We can sincerely believe the Earth isn't round and be sincerely wrong. Truth is discovered, not invented. Gravity existed before Sir Isaac Newton named it.

> "If I say to you, there is no such thing as truth…is that true?"–Dr. Frank Turek

We need to have a direction to point our moral compass. If I take a compass and glue down the needle so it points to me, what happens when I venture off into the woods?

Knowing the truth is not a license to raise myself above others (I'm saved and you're not) nor employ legalism to support my position.

The truth is, I am just a sinner saved by grace. God willingly put on human skin, lived and died as a man, rose from the dead and is very much alive right now. He did this to rescue us from ourselves. We call this the Good News for a reason, we are literally saved.

So why do we work so diligently to remove the name of our Savior and his teachings from public buildings, common sayings, from our schools, workplaces, businesses and government?

Why has being politically correct become the standard by which we judge our behavior?

Why do we push Jesus away? Why do we want nothing to do with the very being who loves us beyond all comprehension?

As a baby Christian, when I read the passage in Luke 22:44 where Jesus was sweating blood as he prayed in the garden of Gethsemane right before he was arrested, I used to think he was in such a state because he was dreading the agony that was to come, because he was a man, he was afraid.

But slowly I began to realize he was anticipating something far more than the physical, mental and emotional torture that was about to be inflicted upon his humanity. He was about to take on the sin of the world, the shame and guilt of every single person, past, present and future. He was about to experience the most intense spiritual agony possible

Think for a moment how you feel when you've hurt someone you love. You yelled at your child or unloaded on your spouse or a friend, maybe you lied or cheated. We all know how guilt feels, how it weighs us down, steals our joy. Worse, many of us know the pain of shame. Guilt is–I made a mistake. Shame is–I am a mistake.

Guilt and shame can keep us in permanent bondage. We

may try to cover them up, self-medicate with drugs or booze or any number of mind-numbing activities, but they remain, festering under the surface, ready to break loose without warning.

Now try and imagine Jesus feeling all the guilt, all the shame, all the regret of humanity *combined*. He was perfect, sinless and he willingly paid the price for our crap. He wrapped himself in chains so we can shake loose ours. Our chains of regret, of defeat, of fear.

We don't have to live weighed down by the past. We don't have to be defined by our mistakes. Yes, a do-over is possible. It is waiting for us. Right now.

Would you like to be freed? For good?

Throwing off the chains of bondage is simple because once you know the truth it will, indeed, *set you free*.

FINDING WISDOM IN THE MANIPULATION OF MARKETERS

"Marketing is the application of the knowledge of human psychology to the task of persuasion. And what psychology has taught the marketing world is the most powerful persuasion of all takes place not through above-the-board appeals but by directly targeting the emotions."
–David Kupelian, The Marketing of Evil

Nobody likes to be manipulated. We all love to think we are smarter than the marketers and never fall prey to their tactics. It is always the "other guy", the dumb one, who succumbs, not me.

We all like to believe we think for ourselves, but it is getting harder and harder as advertising is becoming more and more insidious.

Have you noticed the ever increasing number of targeted ads on the internet? I recently perused my favorite shoe site and suddenly shoe ads are popping up all over my computer.

Sophisticated technology allows companies you have shown an interest in to subtly hound you to buy their product or service. It is like going to a store to look at towels and having a salesperson follow you waving a washcloth everywhere you go.

For some of us, these tactics are backfiring. We are getting turned off to the very people who are trying to reel us in.

We used to say, "find a need and fill it." Today products are being invented to create a solution for a problem that either doesn't exist or for which they have little or no benefit. Take the ubiquitous hand sanitizers. Viruses are spread mainly via tiny droplets in the air that are sneezed or coughed by someone already infected. Far less commonly they can proliferate by touching an infected surface and then rubbing your eyes and nose. So how exactly do hand sanitizers help keep us safe from the flu if we are breathing infected air?

There has never been a product invented that will make us happy. We all know it. We also know a lot of advertising is a manipulative lie. So why are we still vulnerable to marketers?

The answer is simple. We spend entirely too much time in pursuit of things that don't matter.

There was a stupid saying going around a few years ago: he who dies with the most toys wins. Wins what, exactly?

We know we aren't taking our stuff to heaven. Not our big

houses or our cars or our diamonds. None of it. So why are we in constant pursuit of fleeting, inconsequential stuff?

Are we manipulated on such a subliminal level that we have no awareness of it at all?

That is scary. But it doesn't have to be.

Begin right now to build up your awareness muscles. Learn to question your motivation when you get the urge to buy something you don't need or perhaps even want. You already know what that is; you don't need to hear about it from me or anyone else.

Turn on your "I am being conned" antenna; we all have one.

Stop asking your doctor if _____ is right for you, or worse, for your child. It isn't.

Even if you "have it your way," it's still junk food.

Don't "obey your thirst." Use your head.

Try reading through the book of Proverbs one chapter a day for a month. It contains 31 chapters, one for each day and an extra special one for the ladies. I particularly like *The Message* paraphrase, Eugene Peterson did a great job with the verbiage. Here is a sample to get you started.

> *"Talk to Wisdom as a sister. Treat Insight as your companion. They'll be with you to fend off the Temptress—that smooth-talking-honey-tongued Seductress." Proverbs 7:4-5*

Whether they come disguised as a seducer or a seductress, don't allow yourself to be manipulated by marketers. They have an agenda to fill and they need your help. Just say no and politely but firmly close the door in their faces.

FINDING WISDOM
IN THE WAY I HANDLE MONEY

"And my God will meet all your needs according to the riches of his glory in Christ Jesus."
Philippians 4:19 NIV

"Money doesn't talk. It just walks away quietly."
–Rick Warren

When I was a kid I was told I should never talk about money. I was told the same thing about politics and religion. So I learned to be quiet about my finances; most of us are.

Are we ashamed because we have too little? Or embarrassed because we have too much?

Could it be that many of us are ashamed about the way we manage our money? Could it be the debt choking us is too painful to talk about?

Or are we afraid we will be judged for the way we handle money?

Money is a tool, nothing more, nothing less. It will not make you happy. Beyond the necessities of life it can buy you a bit of comfort, but that's about all.

Our money, as with everything else, does not belong to us—it is a gift from God. Out of his love and generosity, he provides resources for us to use for his glory, to sustain us and to help others.

God promises he will meet all our needs. Sometimes we confuse needs with greeds.

If you have a refrigerator full of food, clothes on your back and a roof over your head, you are already richer than 75% of the people alive today. Your basic material needs have been met. If you own a car, your are in the top 8% of the wealthiest people in the world. You are rich!

If we learn to view money as a resource to be managed and not a toy to be used in the pursuit of empty, fleeting gratification, we will make better and easier financial decisions.

If you bought a fine bottle of perfume, you would use it sparingly. You would dab it on and inhale the scent and enjoy the sensations in your nose and brain. If you accidentally spilled it, you would be upset because something precious had been wasted.

Your money is just as precious. It can be traded for another T-shirt that will fall apart in the wash, or it can buy a quality shirt that will last and make you feel good every time you wear it. And the shirt will be what it is: clothing. It won't be a reminder of another trip to the mall in an attempt to find a fleeting moment of "happiness".

Have you seen the movie, *The Joneses*? The main character, Steve, has a neighbor, Larry. Larry buys a new car and shows it to Steve. He is so excited. He loves his car. A short time later, Steve gets a new car. Suddenly the car Larry loved so much pales in comparison to Steve's snazzy new ride. It just isn't so cool anymore. The money Larry spent, or rather borrowed as he didn't have the cash, isn't giving him what he wants. The car didn't change; it's exactly the same, still shiny and new. Larry is let down because he used money to try and buy happiness and a firm identity and it didn't work. It never does.

Money can't buy you identity. True identity is found only in Christ.

So how do we make good financial decisions?

We begin by returning to God our first fruits, the first 10% of the money he has given us.

> *"Bring the whole tithe into the storehouse that there may be food in my house. Trust me in this says the Lord almighty and see if I will not throw open the floodgates of heaven and pour out so much blessing that you will not have room enough for it."*
> *Malachi 3:10 NIV*

Don't you just love this verse? This is the only place in scripture that God says, "put me to the test." God promises that if we are obedient and trust him with our money, we will be blessed. He doesn't need our money, he simply wants us to be obedient with the one thing that seems to dominate our lives. And he never, ever breaks a promise.

I want some of that, don't you?

> *"The rich rule over the poor and the borrower is servant to the lender." Proverbs 22:7 NIV*

We live in a society where instant gratification rules. We are trillions of dollar in debt because we want it all now and think we can have it through the magic of those little plastic cards.

When we are in debt, we are literally in bondage. Instead of tithing and saving and paying our living expenses and sharing and then enjoying some of our well earned cash, we give 18% or more a year to a bank or credit card company. If you want a case of instant depression, add up all the money you have spent over the years in credit card fees and interest. It won't be fun.

I have lived in debt and I have lived debt free. Guess which one is better?

> *"The wise man saves for the future but the foolish man spends whatever he gets." Proverbs 21:20 TLB*

My parents were savers. The only debt they ever had was their mortgage. I grew up in a nice house, not fancy, but well-kept and in a safe neighborhood. We were never hungry. I had nice clothes, not the latest fashion but always neat and clean.

Now you may be thinking, money management is easy for her, she had good role models and good training.

Wrong.

As soon as I left home I started spending money as if there was no tomorrow. I racked up thousands of dollars in debt on clothes and a stereo and records and concert tickets and you name it. I was having fun! Of course the fun stopped once a month when the bills came but the rest of the time I was having a ball. I was throwing away piles of money in interest, but I didn't care. I was young and having a great time spending, spending, spending.

Yes, my parents tithed and saved and lived debt free and that is good, very good. But they never taught me the joy of saving and the rewards that come with good money management. All I saw as a kid was deprivation, and it was no fun at all. It wasn't so much that I didn't understand the rewards of saving—I had some money in the bank and I liked that. It wasn't even that I wanted more stuff. I just wanted some enjoyment from the labor I saw all around me. My parents both worked hard and they could have afforded a bit of fun now and then. But they lived with an attitude of scarcity even though there was enough.

Let's say I got an allowance of $10 a week. $1 goes back to God. $5 goes into the bank and $4 is left for me to use as I want. What if my parents had modeled that once I tithed and saved and paid my living expenses (sharing with me just how much it costs for housing and food, etc.), then I could save for a treat. I needed help in learning how to keep money in its place.

Those of you raising a family or planning to, please teach your kids about money. Model for them good, Godly money management. Teach them early how to earn, tithe, save, share and spend. Show them that God gave them resources to be managed responsibly and for their enjoyment.

> *"Plan carefully and you will have plenty; if you act too quickly, you will never have enough."*
> *Proverbs 21:5 TEV*

Every time we spend, we are investing in something. Investments can be wise or they can be foolish.

If I buy stock in a company, I am betting the company will do well and my money will grow.

If I send my kids to college, I am hoping their education will provide them with a valuable career and a good income.

If I give money to a charity, I am investing in the welfare of another human being.

On the other hand, if I spend $2 on a coffee every morning instead of making it myself at home for a $1, I am investing $1 in my convenience. Unless I have an ownership stake in the coffee shop, I'll never see that $1 again. If I meet a friend there and we sit together and chat over our coffees, then the money was well spent.

What about gambling, playing the lottery? When I buy the ticket, the odds of me winning are minuscule. I am investing in chance. Is that a good investment?

We all like to spend, we like to buy a good time. As I learned growing up, being miserly is not the answer. Spending in and of itself is not bad as long as it is intentional. Impulsive buying is the easiest way for your money to steal off into the night before you even notice.

So, memorize TSPSE:

Tithe, save, pay expenses, share and then enjoy. Even if you can only afford a tiny treat, it will be sweet indeed if you can *truly* afford it, and especially if you won't see it on a bill at the end of the month!

FINDING WISDOM
IN PRACTICING INTEGRITY

"If you pray to God and seek the favor of the Almighty, if you are pure and live with complete integrity, God will rise up and restore your happy home. And though you started with little, you will end up with much." Job 8:5-7 NLT

A man and woman stopped at a fast food drive through to get some chicken. It was getting close to closing time and the manager was cleaning out the cash registers. He saw the car pull up and put the money into a chicken bucket and then filled the order. The kid at the window grabbed the wrong bucket and the couple drove off. Ten minutes later they came back. The manager was so amazed at their honesty he wanted to take their photo and thank them publicly on Facebook. Oh no, the man said quietly, you can't do that. You see, I'm married and the woman I'm with is not my wife.

Have you ever thought about the word integrity? It is the

state of being whole and undivided. The Latin root of the word integer implies the wholeness and consistency of character in a person.

The opposite of being integrated is compartmentalized, divided, split into pieces.

If I say I am faithful to my spouse every day except Tuesday, then I am unfaithful. It's like being a little bit pregnant.

I think most of us want to have integrity. We want to be thought of as trustworthy and dependable.

Keeping my commitments, being on time—I want to, I really do. But I'm just so blasted busy!

Why do so many of us have intimacy and trust issues? Why can't we let anyone get close? We run or push them away before they have a chance to hurt or betray us. Were the adults that surrounded us growing up leading integrated lives?

Integrity leaves a legacy. Children who are surrounded by trustworthy adults learn to live honestly. Kids whose parents are working on their own stuff, who are striving to be authentic and transparent, learn to trust.

But kids who are repeatedly disappointed by broken promises, whose feelings are continually set aside, learn that depending on others is a risk they are willing to take less and less.

The most truly self-confident people I know have two things

in common: they are humble and they have integrity. They are dependable. They keep their promises. They go about their lives with quiet assurance. People speak well of them; they have excellent reputations.

Consistency is critical; it is where reputations are born. We are evaluated and judged by the behavior we employ most often. We all leave a lasting impression whether we realize it or not.

Oh you know how so and so is—she never returns my calls. Oh don't worry about him—he's always late.

I sometimes wonder whether we have too many opportunities. I have a friend who is chronically late, and when I asked her why she said, I just have so many important things to do.

God does not expect us to do everything; only he can.

Not all opportunities are good; they must be carefully evaluated. My motivation must be brought humbly before the Lord. I must ask God whether this venture, this project, this idea is the best use of my time, energy and resources in this season of life.

It is impossible to have integrity and keep our commitments when we say yes for the wrong reasons. Yes to please people, yes out of guilt, yes because everyone else is nodding away and we don't want to stand out.

Another friend of mine, who is self employed, told me people are amazed at the amount of work he is able to do in a short time. He says most people think commitment is saying yes to one thing, when in fact it is often saying no—no to all the other things that seek to distract from the very thing he agreed to do.

Practicing integrity is easier when you learn when and how to say no with kindness and respect.

Integrity is also built by the refusal to gossip. A person with integrity keeps confidences, they can be trusted not to repeat secrets. They don't listen to others being maligned. They don't disguise gossip in the form of a "prayer request."

Integrity is found in less, talking less, listening more. Making thoughtful commitments and keeping them. Using all the various forms of communication to actually communicate.

Let your yes be yes and your no, kindly, be no. Do as you say, say as you do.

Treat the low as the high and the high as the low. In God's eyes, a king is a pauper and a pauper is a king.

A person of integrity is the same alone as they are in a crowd.

And when you occasionally fall short—and you will—start again. Always remember to hold yourself and others accountable with a large spoonful of sweet grace—it truly does help the medicine go down.

FINDING WISDOM
IN SHARING THE GOOD NEWS

"I have told you all this so you have peace with me.
Here on earth you will have many trials and sorrows.
But take heart because I have overcome the world."
John 16:33 NLT

Laura is a wonderful woman in my Bible study small group who used to be an atheist. She has a friend who is a Christian. Her friend has had many difficulties, as we all do while living in this broken world. She has challenges and adversities in her life. She isn't exempt from pain.

Laura said she used to watch her friend deal with her problems. When she walked through the storms of life—illness, the death of a loved one—she wouldn't fret. Laura would ask, "Aren't you worried?" and her friend would say, "No, because I have given it all over to Jesus. He is carrying my burdens and pain and fear for me. I trust that he will deal with everything so I don't have to." Laura was so impressed with the way her friend was modeling her faith that she asked how she could get such peace in her heart, too.

I asked Laura recently whether her friend ever tried to "convert" her. I asked if she ever "preached" or "witnessed" to her. The answer was no.

Laura simply saw something in her friend that was different. She saw the quiet assurance that she wasn't going through life alone, that she had the mighty power of God on her side and no matter what, he would work everything out for good. She saw that her friend had *hope*.

My friend Laura is no longer an atheist. She is a follower of Christ.

I mentioned *The Purpose Driven Life* earlier. At the time of this writing, according to Publisher's Weekly, it is the best selling non-fiction hardback in history—next to the Bible.

Why is it so popular and why have so many people read it? Because it answers the single most important question in life: what on earth am I here for?

You are here because God created you for the sole purpose of loving you. He wanted a family and he wants you in it.

He has five purposes for your life. We all love the first four:

1. You are here to worship God.

2. You are here to be in fellowship with other believers.

3. You are here to be discipled to learn to become more like Christ.

4. You are here to serve God and others.

But then there's number five:

You are here to share the good news. You are here to tell of the hope just waiting for us in Christ.

Oh boy. How do I do it? What do I say?

Perhaps, like Laura's friend, you show more than you speak.

When she was a kid my friend Mary's mom used to tell her, "Your actions are speaking so loudly I can't hear a word you're saying."

What if your actions were speaking so loudly people would be irresistibly drawn to hear you? Did you know you are the first Bible some people will ever read? What do you want them to find in your pages?

In today's culture followers of Christ are being carefully watched. We are belittled, often told we are naive or stupid for believing that Jesus is the son of God. We are told that science has the answer to all the world's problems and as soon as we're smart enough and evolved enough, we'll get it all figured out and fixed.

We have more ways to share information, more tools and technology to explore the mysteries of life than ever before. We have more, more, more of everything. We should be more productive, more fulfilled and happier than ever with all the vast resources within our reach.

And yet we aren't.

Many of us are depressed and anxious. Most of us are exhausted. Even with our vast stores of knowledge and information we still aren't at peace with ourselves and others. We are still in conflict. We are still at war with each other. We are still intolerant. We still grab for power and money and hold on tight.

Why?

Choices. We are eating food that doesn't nourish us. We are filling our time with activities that have little value. We are trying to keep up with the latest and greatest…just trying to keep up, period. We are fixing our minds on sounds and images that desensitize our hearts. The further we reach, the more elusive the answers become.

I know this because I have lived it. I have spent more years than I care to admit chasing after things that don't matter. No matter what I accomplished, no matter how many goals I achieved, there was always something else lurking around the corner. I couldn't get no satisfaction. And I tried and I tried and I tried and I tried.

There is a God-shaped void in all of us. God created us in order to be his beloved children and until we accept that love, we are never whole. Until we look at the cross and realize God was willing to leave heaven, a perfect place, and come to earth and engage in all the messiness, ugliness and uselessness of human life, we will always be searching for something, anything, to fill the hole.

When you get it, that you are loved and valued and esteemed beyond all comprehension, then the good news of Jesus will ooze from your pores. You will not be able to stop loving. You will not be able to stop serving. You will not be able to stop reaching out to the least and the lost.

Like Laura's friend, your life will shine like a beacon and people will notice. They will want to know what is driving you, what is your "secret"?

And with great joy you can tell them all about how the King of the Universe is your best friend, and he wants to be their BFF, too.

He longs to fill our hearts with peace and love and...*hope*.

Get on your knees and thank your creator for making you. Thank him for dying so you don't have to. Accept the gift of joy and peace he gives you without reservation.

Then get up and go build the kingdom.

And remember:

> *We are all just beggars showing another beggar where to find the food.*

FINDING WISDOM
IN FORGIVENESS

"Be kind to one another, tenderhearted, forgiving one another as God forgave you." Ephesians 4:32 ESV

The concept of forgiveness is a difficult and painful subject for so many of us. Whether we struggle with forgiving others who have wronged us or with forgiving ourselves, the idea of truly letting go is perplexing and confusing and just plain hard.

Some of us struggle with thinking we haven't forgiven if we still remember the pain. Not true. Healing takes time. What we can do is stop ruminating on the hurt, stop chewing on it. We can turn our minds to other things, to what is pure and noble and lovely, as Paul says in Philippians 4:8.

Others of us think if the relationship isn't fully restored then we haven't truly forgiven. Not necessarily. Abusive relationships may never be restored as long as the abuser runs away from God.

Or we may think forgiveness equals trust, so when we still feel wary, are we carrying a grudge? No. Trust has to be rebuilt over time with a sincere and consistent change in behavior on the part of the offender.

You will know when there is genuine forgiveness in your heart this way: true forgiveness is found by wishing the person who has hurt you no ill, by hoping they do well and by sincerely praying they will grow to know Jesus better. You will want them free from bondage, because an unrepentant heart is a heart in chains.

Remember, the person who hurt you and isn't truly sorry is not at peace. They may look okay on the surface, but underneath there is unresolved pain and conflict festering in their heart and in their mind.

When we have been hurt, it takes time to heal, especially if the person has not truly apologized, just mumbled a fake "I'm sorry" and then gone on to repeat the hurtful behavior.

It is easier to forgive when the apology is sincere. Just as Jesus forgives us instantly when we humble ourselves before him and confess, we can, too.

If my friend hurts me and doesn't realize it and as soon as I tell her she sincerely apologizes, then we are ready to move forward. Even if the hurt doesn't go away immediately, the healing process has begun and the pain has lost its power.

But what happens when we're hurt and the offender has no remorse, takes no responsibility or, worse, turns the blame on us? What if we simply cannot find the means to forgive?

I had a painful childhood. I was adopted at birth and my parents, although well intentioned, were wounded and broken themselves and, as a result, emotionally distant. Although they professed to be followers of Christ, went to church, said and did all the right things in public, they were both lonely and bitter people. I grew up in a house full of gossip and the constant judging of the people around us who never quite measured up. My parents would fight and my father would try and get me to side with him against my mother. Psychologists call this enmeshment and it is devastating to a child.

My father died when I was 14, and my mother turned to me for comfort. In her grief she looked to an immature teenager to bind her wounds and make her whole. More enmeshment. Instead of turning to the Lord and other adults for help, she turned to me.

When I would want to go out with a friend she would cry or worse, pretend it was okay and then sulk. She wanted 100% of my attention all the time. I am a sensitive person, and I felt so guilty for wanting a life of my own that I had what I guess you would call a nervous breakdown. I felt such overwhelming guilt and shame for not being able give up my dreams of a life for myself that I was drowning inside. I got no help from anyone; even my aunts and uncles told me I had to take care of my mother.

For over a year I barely left the house. I knew I was in serious trouble and asked to see a therapist. My mother said therapists were crazier than their patients, but I insisted.

I was blessed to find a psychologist who listened to me with great empathy. I had never been truly listened to before in my life. My mother was jealous of the affection I had for my therapist and tried to get me to stop seeing her, but I refused. Then she went to talk to the doctor herself and told me the doctor said I was to be a good daughter and take care of my mother who needed me. When I told my therapist, she just shook her head and said, no, that was not what I said. I told your mother to seek professional counsel and help from other adults.

Looking back now, I realize how much pain my mother must have been in.

During that very bad year, the school district sent a home teacher who was very kind to me. She would often close the books we were supposed to be studying and just talk with me. We talked about many different things, and she told me I was very intelligent and had a great future. She and my therapist lifted me out of a dark, dark place, and I am forever grateful.

But the residual damage from all the trauma was my inability to form healthy relationships. I lived in constant fear of having my reality scorned, of being of no value unless I was giving up myself for the needs of another. I didn't understand the give and take of a healthy relationship and I felt awash in shame.

My heavenly father knew all about the trouble I was in and sent two angels to help me. First Mary and then Leonard.

I used to spend a lot of time at Mary's house with her husband and daughters. My mother didn't like Mary because she knew I loved her. At Mary's house I was treated with respect and affection. I was allowed to be myself. And not only that, just being me was okay; I was even admired.

Then Mary introduced me to Leonard, the first and only blind date I ever went on. I don't know about love at first sight, but I instantly felt a connection. There was something about this guy, and I wanted to find out just what. And in short order I knew he was the *one*.

My mother sensed it right away. And pretty soon she knew she was beaten.

Yet she never gave up the fight. She continued to remind me that if only I would do this or be that, then she would be happy. She never stopped believing that another human being could save her. Afraid I would have another breakdown, I saw her rarely, mostly at family gatherings. Holidays were torture, but I gritted my teeth, smiled and got through them.

Finally I just couldn't take it any longer. The pressure to make her happy was breaking me. During the last two years of her life I made sure she was well taken care of, that her needs were met, that she was comfortable but that was all I could do. I cared about her but I wasn't strong enough to be around her. I didn't know Jesus so I had to try and cope on my own. It's difficult to write these words, but they are true.

She died in 2005, and at first the only thing I felt was relief. I was able to bury any lingering guilt in the knowledge that she was no longer around to torment me. I use the word torment on purpose, because shame and guilt are torturous.

When I came to know Jesus in 2009 I began to think about how he had forgiven me. I could barely stand to see images of him on the cross (they bother me today but in a different way—now I can never be grateful enough for what he has done for me and he knows that) because his sacrifice was the picture of what forgiveness is. He willingly set himself aside and gave his life to pay the price for my guilt, my shame, my sin. You know how we always tell others to "let it go"? *He let it go for me.*

I began to ask him to help me forgive my mother. I had been praying for sanctification, to grow more like him, to see people the way he does. I thought about the words he said on the cross: "Father forgive them for they don't know what they are doing." I tried to wrap my mind around the idea that Jesus was forgiving his tormentors, his executioners, right in the middle of the most horrific pain imaginable. How he realized they were so broken, so confused, so full of sin that they couldn't see him for who he was: God in human flesh.

So I decided to use his words. I said, "Lord, please forgive her. Go easy on her. She didn't realize what she was doing." There is power in those words. And I asked him to help me forgive her, too. I told him I had tried and tried and just couldn't get there. I really meant it; I had no more trying left in me.

And slowly the steamer trunk of guilt and shame began to empty out. The burden began to lift. It became easier for me to give people grace, to be patient. By tapping into the power of Jesus and his forgiveness, I was able to accept grace, too. The more forgiveness I gave, the lighter I felt.

Now you may be thinking, well, it's okay for her, her mother is dead and she doesn't have to deal with her any longer. And that is true. If I had known Jesus when she was still alive, I would have told her of the change in my heart. I would have encouraged her to turn to the Lord to carry her pain. I would have prayed with her and for her.

But if she had continued to abuse me I would have stayed away, just as I did. Sometimes a relationship cannot be rebuilt. But I was restored and made whole and you can be, too.

I haven't thought about all this in a long time. These days my heart is full of grace, and it overflows into the lives of the people around me. I could never, ever do this on my own. I tried for years to cope and I barely managed that. I couldn't fathom the concept of forgiving my mother and father. Oh, of course I knew I should, but at times I was hurting so badly I really didn't even want to.

Only Jesus was able to soften my heart, and through his great love and sacrifice, I was able to see a glimmer of what it means to forgive. Once I got a taste I wanted more, and he is never stingy.

Forgiveness became a lifestyle for me, because I know, if my hands are clenched in bitterness and resentment, then my palms aren't open to receive God's blessings.

Guilt and shame can be crowded out of your life with the pure love and joy found only in a relationship with your savior, who, while tortured and bleeding to death, *forgave*.

He didn't wait for us to confess. He forgave while we were still deep in sin.

We need to stop trying to "let it go" on our own. I couldn't. Maybe you can't either. We need a professional, someone who is a master at the complex art of forgiveness.

Call on him by name. Write out your grievance and lay it before him. Ask him to file it for you.

Then let him go to work. He's got it covered, and you don't need to keep a copy.

> *"This means that anyone who belongs to Christ has become a new person. The old life is gone; a new life has begun!" 2 Corinthians 5:17 NLT*

> *"When there is a cross on your back, there is no room for a chip on your shoulder." Buddy Owens*

FINDING WISDOM
IN SINNING LESS

"I already know I'm going to hell; at this point its really go big or go home."

"Of course I'm going to hell, that's where all my friends will be and we're going to party hardy!"

For most of us, sin is a big word. It's scary. Nobody wants to be thought of as a sinner. Maybe that's why we make fun of it —deep down it frightens us, and joking helps relieve the tension. In the short term, sin is fun—otherwise, nobody would want to do it.

When we hear the word sin, we think of the Ten Commandments: murder, adultery, lying, not keeping the Sabbath and all the rest. Those are most definitely sins. But what about the fun ones, you know, like gossip and little white lies and puffing myself up by putting someone else down?

Yes, those are sins, too. We all sin; I do; you do. We live in a world broken by sin.

With all the terrible, evil atrocities in the world today, with the rampant corruption right here in our own country, it is easy to focus only on the big bad stuff and forget we are sinning all the time.

I haven't murdered anyone, but I have sinned today. Just a few minutes ago I observed prideful thoughts floating through my mind.

In our culture more and more, sin is made out to be funny.

When we laugh at sin, we are playing Satan's game right alongside him. When we sin, jokingly, with big smiles on our faces, we are influencing the people around us by showing that it's okay, even fun. I don't think most of us are aware, but we're doing it just the same.

Do you know how Satan's game is played?

When he encourages us to sin, he always minimizes the effects. His tactics go something like this: oh come on, it's no big deal, _____ is just a little fun. It won't hurt you. Everybody's doing it and they're fine; you will be, too. Life is short; live a little!

If I say to you, oh go ahead, have that donut, one won't hurt you, I ate one and I'm fine…am I sinning?

Think about it. When we use Satan's verbiage to endorse our sin, who are we aligning ourselves with, God or the enemy?

Satan uses whatever tactics (and he knows the most effective ones) he can to weaken our minds and bodies. The more we allow him to minimize our sin, the stronger his hold on us becomes.

One donut will not make you fat or sick. But many donuts, many sodas, many bags of chips, multiplied over time, can and will.

Buying one new thing you can't afford won't get you into financial bondage, but one after another, over time, will.

Watching one movie full of violence or graphic sex or foul language won't weaken your mind. But many bad movies, songs and video games, over time, will.

Then, after we've given in and done the deed, suddenly Satan changes his tune. Now his song goes: you idiot. Didn't you know that _____ would make you fat? Sick? Cost you that friendship? Your marriage? Put you in debt? What were you thinking? How stupid, dumb, careless, blind, weak could you be?

Suddenly the sin that was so much fun and no big deal is a huge problem, and *nobody's laughing.*

God is a master at long-term thinking. Since he resides outside of time and space, he sees immediately the long-term consequences of our short-term actions.

When we seek to justify our sin using Satan's tactics, I wonder if, as the kind and loving father he is, God shakes his mighty head and quietly pleads with us to turn away, to choose the strawberry instead of the donut.

We cannot control our sinful nature on our own. Period. As with diets, willpower works for a time. But sooner or later something happens, and we don't just fall off the wagon, we fly off at warp speed and land in a big pile of whatever we were trying so hard to avoid.

Yes, we must confess, and of course we are immediately forgiven. But sometimes we forget the part about repenting, turning away from sin. And we forget the part where Jesus said, "Go and sin no more."

Does he know we will sin again? Absolutely. Will he forgive us? Yes, over and over and over. He never runs out of grace. But he actually does us one better: not only will he forgive but he will help us to sin less by giving us his power to stand up under Satan's assaults, and we will not be crushed.

> *"Any temptation you face will be nothing new. But God is faithful and He will not let you be tempted beyond what you can handle. He always provides a way of escape so that you will be able to endure and keep moving forward." 1 Corinthians 10:13 The Voice*

God will keep us moving forward and help us learn from our mistakes.

So how do we learn to sin less?

First, begin to quietly observe your thought patterns. Don't jump right in and judge what you're thinking—just observe. Watch how often you feel pulled to think or do something you know isn't right. Listen to how Satan nudges your heart and helps you justify your sin. You will soon see clearly how the enemy is using your natural tendencies to pervert your nature and draw you into sin. Awareness is the beginning of change. The more you observe, the better you know yourself, the faster you will be able to turn away.

Second, practice the art of substitution. Instead of treating your kids to a donut, buy them some gorgeous organic fruit in season. No kid will turn down fresh strawberries with a dollop of homemade whipped cream. Instead of a chemical-laden frozen yogurt, get a fresh fruit smoothie. If you start when they are very young, you will set them up for a lifetime of good choices.

Save up and buy one pair of fabulous shoes or a great sound system or season tickets to football or the ballet or whatever you love. Don't dwell on the things you don't have; enjoy to the fullest what you've got.

Actively seek entertainments that edify, lift up and espouse the highest values in life and fill your mind with those. They do exist. Support them with your money.

Decide and define once and for all your values and what you stand for. Stop patronizing businesses that promote ideas and products outside your value system.

And always remember: it is so much easier to sin less when your thoughts, feelings and actions are aligned with Jesus.

Putting Christ at the center of your heart and involving him in every decision will help you, almost without effort, to sin much less.

This side of heaven we will never be perfect, so let the Holy Spirit go to work and sanctify you. Don't fight it. Your stress level will drop and you will feel ever so much better about yourself. You have God's iron-clad guarantee.

> *"For sin shall no longer be your master because you are not under the law, but under grace."*
> *Romans 6:14 NIV*

FINDING WISDOM IN THE MOST IMPORTANT THING I WILL EVER LEARN

We love Lucy, but does she know how much?

Our friends Adam and Kristen have a dog named Lucy. She is just about the sweetest, cutest dog God ever made. She often accompanies her mom and dad to our weekly small life group and Bible study. We all feel so blessed by her. She runs in the door so excited to see us, and greets everyone with a doggie kiss. It is impossible not smile at the very sight of her.

Adam suffers from severe depression. Kristen loves and cares for him, and through all their trials their marriage is rock solid. It is truly amazing to see, and they give all the credit to God.

About four years ago, God gave them the gift of Lucy. They weren't looking for a dog. They really didn't want a dog; they couldn't afford a pet.

Lucy was a tiny puppy who had been abandoned and was found wandering through the streets of Los Angeles. She got passed from owner to owner. A vet who treated her said she had lived a lifetime in the first few weeks of her life.

But God had a plan for Lucy. He knew exactly where she was going. He had her family all picked out.

So, through a series of amazing events, Lucy arrived, all shots up to date, with her own crate, bed, leash and a big bag of food. God even took care of the adoption expenses! Funny how he always seems to remember the smallest details.

Adam and Kristen *love* Lucy. They adore this little dog. And she loves them back. But she has no idea how much they love her, how much she means to them, how much she helps them, how much her very presence blesses them. *She has no idea.*

All she knows is that she is well fed, comfortable, warm, petted, cared for, told how adorable she is and loved, loved, loved all the time.

She doesn't understand what her mere existence means to her mom and dad.

About a year after Lucy came to live with her new family, Adam had a severe bout of depression. Very, very bad. He couldn't get out of bed. The urge to end the pain, to end his life, was overwhelming.

Now, normally during the day Lucy likes to have some me-time. Her daddy works from home, so when he is at the computer, she will often go off by herself and think her doggie thoughts. We like to think she is praying.

But on this particular day she stayed on the bed with Adam. As he drifted in and out of sleep he imagined how, soon, he would be out of this horrific pain, this unrelenting darkness. But he didn't do it. He simply couldn't cause Lucy the pain of wondering what happened, where was daddy, why is mommy so sad.

Adam is still here, by the grace of God. He believes Lucy saved his life that day.

> *"The Lord is my shepherd, I have all that I need."*
> *Psalm 23:1 NLT*

One night in our small group we were talking about how we just don't get how much God loves us, and if we did, that one belief would change everything.

Kristen suddenly got very excited and said, "I have to tell you something. The other day Adam and I were talking and he said, 'You know, Lucy is just like us. She has no idea how much we love her, all she knows is that we take care of her, we supply her every need, we love on her constantly. And she is perfectly satisfied even though she doesn't have the brain capacity to understand the depth of human love. And that is exactly how we are with God.'"

Yes! Adam's got it! God is constantly taking care of us, showering us with his love and affection. He is working behind the scenes 24/7 on our behalf. We are his number one priority.

And yet, often we just don't see it. Like Lucy, we don't have the brain capacity to understand that kind of love. But unlike Lucy, we often aren't content in his love; we're not satisfied. We worry. We fear. We envy.

Do we honestly think God's love is limited like ours?

Do we truly think that when God gives us a trial, a lesson designed to teach us a better way, that means he has stopped loving us?

If Lucy is naughty and her mommy or daddy have to tell her so, does she think for a moment they don't love her?

Do we think our faults, our dumb mistakes, yes, our sins, are keeping God at arm's length?

Or maybe we think he doesn't want to get close because, well, if he really *knew* me…guess what, he does. He knows your every thought, your every feeling, your every sin, and it doesn't change the way he loves you one bit. *He will never love you any less or any more than he does at this very moment.*

Lucy gets it.

Even though she didn't start out well, like some of us, and even though she has little scars on her psyche, like many of us, once she joined her new, loving family and accepted the love that was being offered to her, she began to heal. Today she is happy and healthy.

The most important thing you will ever learn is that you are called to be loved by God. He created you for the sole purpose of loving you.

When we get it, when we realize that we are loved not for what we do or who we are, but for simply existing, then our healthy self-esteem rises, our insecurities dissolve and we become the person God created us to be.

All of us long for family, for connection. That is how God longs for you. He wants you in his family so badly. He wants to adopt you right now, this minute.

Say it out loud: I am a unique, beloved child of God and he created me for the sole purpose of loving me!

Just like Lucy.

Lucy was sent to my friends to give them comfort and solace and peace and joy.

God sent Jesus to give you all those things and more, something Lucy can't give. He sent his son to give you eternal life through the price he paid so you don't have to.

We all know John 3:16, the most famous verse in the Bible:

> *"For God so loved the world that he gave his one and only son so that whoever believes in him shall not perish but have eternal life." NIV*

Eternal life. Forever life. Life without end.

One day your life here on earth will come to a close and your real life will begin. A beautiful life full of joy. No pain, no suffering, a perfect life in a perfect place.

God wants you there with him. Adam and Kristen's love for Lucy reconciled her to the human race. Jesus wants the same for you, to be reconciled with your creator. All you have to do is believe in him. Let him take care of you, Lean on his wisdom. Embrace the love he showers on you. Be a willing receiver of the greatest love of all.

Be like Lucy.

OKAY, I GET IT

Okay, I get it. My choices govern my life; my everyday decisions determine my future. I know I should take care of my body. I know I should talk less, listen more, be more generous, kind, thrifty. Hey, that story about the dog is cute. I know love is the answer. The Beatles said it: all you need is love.

But you know, sometimes I am just not feeling it. Sometimes I know what I should do and I don't—and I just don't care.

It is easy to talk about love and wisdom in the abstract. It is easy to feel loving toward our friends and family. It's another story entirely to talk about loving our enemies, doing good to those who hate us. On our own we cannot manufacture that kind of love. We need to tap into the source of lasting love and ultimate wisdom.

As I write these words, we all have lived through a year of evil atrocities both here at home and around the world. I don't need to recap the terrorist attacks, the shootings, the violence, man's inhumanity against man.

I don't know the specific pain in a person's heart that would cause them to commit these horrific crimes. I don't know the problems in your life, I don't know what you are struggling with, I can't feel your pain. But I do know this: Every problem in life stems from a broken relationship with our heavenly father.

The worst negative effect on a person's life and on a society as a whole is, by far, an absentee or neglectful or abusive father. A broken or dysfunctional relationship with your dad will impact everything in your life.

I know. I have lived it.

If poor parenting from your dad or no dad at all wreaks havoc on us as individuals, what happens to our world when we have no relationship with our heavenly father who created us, *without whom we would not exist?*

The story of the Bible is the story of two characters: us and God. Us and our dad.

Our daddy, God, is seeking us, over and over, because he wants a relationship with his kids. As in the book of Genesis, chapter 3, he wants to walk and talk with us in the cool of the day; but like Adam and Eve, we hide from him. They wanted what he gave them, a gorgeous garden and delicious food—and each other—but they didn't want him.

Ever since Adam and Eve, there is a part of us that feels that way toward God. We want to do whatever we choose and we don't want to have to worry about what he thinks. We don't want him to cramp our style. Yeah, yeah, I know you love me, whatever. Go away. I'm busy living my life and I'm doing just fine.

Our default reaction to the love of God is not to be comforted or embraced by it but to be annoyed.

Every religion except Christianity explains the fact that we can't see or touch God by saying he keeps his distance because he is mad at us. He's disappointed in us. He's too busy. He doesn't like what we've been doing and so he left. If I want a relationship with him, it's up to me to appease him, to beg for his favor. Maybe, just maybe, if I can get his attention, he'll love me. And then again, maybe he won't.

Jesus, and his willingness to carry the sin of the world, gave us a human picture of God's love for us. Just as we never stop loving our kids, no matter what they do, God never takes his love away—it never runs out, it never fails.

The reason the Bible is so long is because God wouldn't give up on us.

For thousands of years, God tried again and again to draw his children close to him. Some of them came and stayed, most hung around for a while but sooner or later dumped him for something bright and shiny, like the three-year-olds we talked about earlier.

Finally, in what must have been a moment of the greatest frustration possible, God did the unthinkable: he became one of us. If we wouldn't go to him, he would come to us.

Jesus is what it looks like for God to *relentlessly* pursue us.

He wanted his family with him just that badly.

And what did we do? We killed him. We said to God: "We told you we didn't want you, which part don't you understand?"

And as far as we were concerned, that was that.

But he didn't stay dead. He is very much alive right this very moment. And you know what that means? It means he can take whatever we throw at him, bounce back and keep on loving us. He never quits no matter what.

If you have or ever had small children, you may have heard, "I want _____." "No, you can't have _____." "But I want it!" "The answer is still no." "You are so mean, I hate you!"

You didn't like it but you could handle it. You could take it because you were bigger than them. And you could take it because you knew saying no in that moment was in the child's best interest. You said no out of your deep love for your baby. You said no to protect them, to help them, to teach them. *To keep them from harm.*

And later on, after the storm had passed and you reminded them how much you love them, they may have said, "Yes, I already know that. Now leave me alone." But deep down, you knew they didn't mean it.

Maybe deep inside, when we push God away, we don't mean it either.

God is bigger than us and he can take it. And then ask quietly, again, for us to return to the fold where he can love and protect us.

We all know the story of the prodigal son. In asking for his inheritance early and going off to have fun, he was, in essence, saying to his father, I want your money but I don't want you.

Then, after he had blown up his life completely and was starving, literally, and living with pigs, he hit rock bottom and sought help from his dad. He was too ashamed to ask for his place in the family back. He simply wanted to be a servant, not just so he could have regular meals, but more importantly so he would once again have a place to belong.

We all know what happened: not only did his father welcome him home, he treated him like royalty, giving him the best of everything he had because he was overjoyed to have his baby home.

If you read this parable carefully, you may notice something: when the son tries to apologize, saying he has sinned and is no longer fit to be called a son, the father doesn't even hear him, because he is so busy giving orders to the servants to bring him the finest robe and a signet ring (the credit card of the day) for his son and to start preparing a grand welcome home party.

He doesn't care what the kid did, he just wants him back.

This story does far more than relate to my life. This story does far more than relate to your life. This story does far more than relate to our world.

*This story is my life. And it is **yours.***

You know God, it would be great if I could have your money without having you. I could take all the wonderful things you have made for me—my inheritance, and you know, like food and sex and art and music and family and friends (and cute clothes and shoes), and I'll take the good things and go live my life because I can enjoy it all a lot more if you're not around.

This pretty much described me. Maybe it describes you, too.

There are two kinds of people in the world: Those who have run out of money and those who haven't.

The prodigal son does not return home until his wallet is empty.

Money is a metaphor for trying it all, achieving your dreams and goals—living large—and realizing, in the end, you didn't feel the way you thought you would. Something was missing.

Some of you have bank accounts that are still bulging, so you don't need Jesus. You might even belittle him. You might mock people who call him their Lord and Savior.

He can take it.

He might embarrass you, that whole gruesome business with the cross might make you uncomfortable.

He doesn't care. He bled for you, too.

Unlike the gods and goddesses of myth, he doesn't fight and curse and take his wrath out on you. He loves you. He wants you. Now.

But what about the evil in the world? What about hell? If he loves me so much, why am I suffering? Why doesn't he step in and stop it all? For me and for everybody else?

Our world is broken by sin. Every time we make a choice, a decision, that goes against the good God has for us, we crack it a little more.

God wants us to be agents of reconciliation. He wants us to be peacemakers.

He hates what is happening to his beloved children on the beautiful planet he created for them to enjoy. He grieves our sin. He hates it. And one day he will put a stop to it.

There will be no peace on earth until the Prince of Peace reigns.

In the meantime, each of us must decide which way to go, toward God or away from him.

If you choose to turn away, you can. Love is a choice. God will not force you to love him. As with the prodigal son's dad, he will let you leave. He will grieve the loss of his precious child but he will let you go.

One day we all will die. 100% guaranteed, you and I will die. And if you don't want to be in God's family, he will honor your wishes. He won't contest your will.

You will be separated for eternity from God and all the wonderful gifts he lavishes on his kids: love, happiness, peace, joy, fun, generosity, gentleness, beauty, kindness, *hope*.

Without him you will be left with the things that aren't his: hatred, bigotry, racism. Envy. Impatience. Thoughtlessness. Pride. Greed. Lust. Not love, lust. You will use and you will be used. You won't care about anybody and *no one will ever care about you*.

Eternal separation from God and his goodness. A sobering thought to be sure.

Many of us are living in a state of low-grade fear all the time. Fear for our country, fear for our planet, fear for our loved ones and fear for ourselves. But we don't have to be like little kids who are scared of the dark. We don't have to be afraid anymore.

We don't even have to have great faith: we just need faith in the right person.

Because, when God is for us, who can be against us?

Our faith will help us grow up. We can become spiritually mature. God will give us vision to see the world the way he does. He will show us a heavenly perspective.

Spiritual maturity in Christ is not found in separating from society, climbing to the top of a mountain, growing a long beard and meditating all day long. Spiritual maturity is found in getting our hands dirty, getting involved in the messiness of life. Getting involved in the pain of others. Lifting up the lost and the least. And then standing back and watching the blessings flow.

We will start to see God reveal his power and might in a

thousand different ways every single day. We will know that, in fact, the world is not spinning out of control, but that it is being held, lovingly, and with great sadness, in the palm of his mighty hand.

We will begin to see that the source of all our problems is simply our self-imposed distance from God. And we will yearn, with all our hearts, to draw ever closer to him. Then our fear will turn to peace.

We can change our default state from annoyance to acceptance by allowing ourselves to be embraced by the greatest lover there ever was. And is.

Make the wisest choice of all. Don't just choose life here on earth. Choose *abundant* life forever. Choose Jesus.

And the wisdom you've been searching for will be yours —shiny and brand new, just waiting to be unwrapped.

Note: This chapter was inspired and informed by "The Annoying Love of God" a sermon by Ryan Holladay, lead pastor at Lower Manhattan Community Church. May God bless you richly, Ryan, as you share the love of Jesus with the people of New York City.

CLOSING PRAYER

Dear Heavenly Father,

Thank you for the precious person who has read this book. Thank you for loving them so much you sent your one and only son to pay their debt and set them free.

May they understand that you love them beyond all comprehension and know without a doubt you have a grand plan and purpose for their life.

Please grant them the wisdom to go forward on their journey with you and make great choices.

And Father, I ask one day to have the pleasure of meeting them in heaven.

I pray this with great gratitude in Jesus' name,

Amen

A LAST WORD FROM
YOUR HEAVENLY FATHER

*"You'll find me when you get serious about finding me and
want it more than anything else."*
Jeremiah 29:13 The Message

And you will…

"Rise to the heights! Live full lives in the fullness of God."
Ephesians 3:19 The Message

ACKNOWLEDGMENTS

I would like to thank all the wonderful people who have contributed directly or indirectly to the writing of this book.

For simply being who you are, my family:

Frank and Melissa Colson
Jared Colson
Nick and Allison Colson and Clara Marie
Trey Colson
Sophia Colson
Timothy Colson
Paul Colson
Caleb Colson
Nila Colson
Nadia Colson

For their prayers and encouragement along the way:

Paige Boots
Maddy Clemens
Linda Crighton
Patti Droesch
Heather Gennette
Andrea Hall
Apryll Held
Laura Mamakos
Denise Martinez
Solange Montoya
Summer Powers
Tina Price
Adam, Kristen and Lucy Weitz
Robin Whitmore
Cindy Whittaker
Ron and Faye Wilbur

For all they have taught me:

Dr. Kathy Camarillo

Pastor Tom Holladay
Pastor John Ortberg
Pastor Buddy Owens

A special thanks to my editor, Shawn Mihalik of Asymmetrical Press. He shepherded this first-time writer through the editing process with great care. His skill shines through every page. Books truly come alive in the editing, and I am blessed to have Shawn help give life to this one.

And saving the best for last, my dearest friend, Mary Rellez. Over the last 40-plus years of our friendship, I have watched her shower love, encouragement and grace everywhere she goes. She truly cares about people. She has put the needs of others before her own more times than I can remember. I have never heard an unkind word spoken about her, and that is quite a feat. She has had more than her share of sorrow and pain, and yet she always looks for the good in everything and everyone. She has given me a higher education in the art of friendship. She, like Leonard, has stuck by me through thick and thin, and I am blessed to call her my friend. I love you, Mare.

WITH HEARTFELT THANKS

To Pastor Rick and Kay Warren, without whose love, influence and care this book would not exist. I came to know Jesus as a result of reading *The Purpose Driven Life*, and a year later, Leonard did, too. In 2011 we sold our home in Connecticut and moved 3000 miles to join Saddleback Valley Community Church where we have been loved, taught, discipled and walked alongside with by some of the best people you will ever meet. Our lives are changing dramatically as we grow to know Jesus better and better, and Rick and Kay and our church family have been a huge part of that growth.

I want to publicly thank these two loving, courageous, Godly people for the difference they and their ministry have made in our lives. I have watched them endure personal tragedy and I have seen them use their unspeakable pain for the good of others. I have seen them, over and over, share selflessly, with unshakable faith, all they have learned in forty-five plus years of ministry.

But most of all, I have watched them, day after month after year, do all they do for one reason only:

To reach one more for Jesus.

To our beloved Rick and Kay: count us on that list.

GET IN THE GROOVE WITH YOUR CREATOR

If you aren't familiar with current praise and worship music, you're in for a tasty treat. There are some amazing artists out there who are writing and performing the most beautiful music. These are not your father's *How Great Thou Art*—although that is a classic. Here are a few to get you started:

Rising Sun
All Sons and Daughters
Paul Mabury, Kyle Lee, David Leonard, Leslie Jordan

Open Up the Heavens
Meredith Andrews

God I Look to You
Bethel Live
Jenn Johnson, Ian McIntosh

No Longer Slaves
Jonathan David Helser and Melissa Helser
Brian Johnson, Jonathan David Helser, Joel Case

Shout to the Lord
Hillsong Church
Darlene Zschech

The Desert Song
Hillsong United
Brooke Fraser

From the Inside Out
Hillsong United
Joel Houston

O Praise The Name (Anástasis)
Hillsong United
Dean Ussher, Marty Sampson, Benjamin Hastings

Oceans (Where Feet May Fail)
Hillsong United
Joel Houston, Matt Crocker, Salomon Lightheim

The Stand
Hillsong United
Natalie Stewart, Salem Brown, Nolan Dion Weekes

With Everything
Hillsong United
Joel Houston

The Creed
Hillsong Worship
Ben Fielding, Matt Crocker

The Revelation Song
 Kari Jobe
Jennie Lee Riddle

Heart Like You
Love and the Outcome
Joel King, Chris Rademaker, Seth Jones

All is Well
Robin Mark
Johnny Parks, Claire Hamilton

Healing Grace
Rick Muchow

Let It Be Jesus
Christy Nockels
Chris Tomlin, Jonas Marin, Matt Redman

God Is In Control
Twila Paris

10,000 Reasons
Matt Redman
Jonas Myrin, Matt Redman

Careless (Song of Dependence)
Saddleback Church Worship
Socrates Perez, Temree Abajian

Your Will Be Done
Saddleback Church Worship
Socrates Perez

Good Good Father
Chris Tomlin
Pat Barrett, Anthony Bowen

How Can I Keep From Singing
Chris Tomlin.
Ni Bhraonain, Eithne Ryan, Nicky Ryan, Roma Shane

Lord I Need You
Chris Tomlin
Christy Nockels, Daniel Carson, Jesse Reeves, Kristian Stanfill, Matt Mahen

Whom Shall I Fear (God of Angel Armies)
Chris Tomlin
Ed Cash, Scott Cash, Chris Tomlin

Praise the King
Corey Voss
Corey Voss, Dustin Smith, Michael Farren, Michael Bryce, Jr.

Hello My Name Is
Matthew West

This Is Amazing Grace
Phil Wickham
Phil Wickham, Josh Farro, Jeremy Riddle

Turned out to be more than a few! I had trouble stopping as there are so many. Listen, sing along in worship and enjoy.

SUGGESTED READING

In today's busy world, many of us are missing out on the wonderful gift of books. We simply have no time to read. Fortunately we have audiobooks. I am a voracious reader, and more and more I find myself reaching for my iPod or my phone. I listen to books while walking, while doing housework, while cooking. If you don't have time to sit down and read, I highly suggest a subscription to an audiobook service. You will re-discover, or maybe discover for the first time, the joy of reading.

I am always searching for wisdom and have found some shiny nuggets in the books listed below:

Wheat Belly
William Davis, MD

Love and Respect
Emerson Eggerichs

I Don't Have Enough Faith to Be an Atheist
Norman L. Geisler, Frank Turek

Beloved Dust
Jamin Goggin and Kyle Strobel

Life on Mission
Tim Harlow

Love-Powered Parenting
Tom and Chaundel Holladay

Chasing Cool
Noah Kerner, Gene Pressman

The Life-Changing Magic of Tidying Up
Marie Kondo

How Evil Works
David Kupelian

The Marketing of Evil
David Kupelian

Mere Christianity
C.S. Lewis

Everything That Remains
Joshua Fields Millburn, Ryan Nicodemus

Minimalism: Live a Meaningful Life
Joshua Fields Millburn, Ryan Nicodemus

The Way of a Worshiper
Buddy Owens

Food Rules
Michael Pollan

Saving Your Marriage Before It Starts
Drs. Les and Leslie Parrott

The Case for Christianity Answer Book
Lee Strobel

The Case for Faith
Lee Strobel

Stealing from God
Frank Turek

Life Without Limits
Nick Vujicic

Stuffocation
James Wallman

The Daniel Plan
Rick Warren, Daniel Amen, Mark Hyman

The Purpose Driven Life
Rick Warren

Prayer
Philip Yancey

And finally, you truly cannot read the Bible too often. As we grow in our journey with Christ, the Holy Spirit reveals more and more of the wisdom contained in the pages. Even if you've read a passage repeatedly, even if you have it memorized, something new will be revealed to you when God decides it is time. Never let a day go by without opening the greatest book ever written, the owner's manual for life. The Bible Gateway app is a great tool. You can easily read, side by side, the same passage in multiple translations. Read or listen to your Bible and hear what God has to say to you *today*.

BIBLE TRANSLATIONS USED IN THIS BOOK

AMP The Amplified Bible
Zondervan (1965)

ESV English Standard Version
Crossway Bibles (2001)

The Message
Nav Press (1993)

MEV Modern English Version
Passio Charisma House (2014)

NET New English Translation
Biblical Studies Press (2005)

NIV New International Version
Zondervan (2011)

NLT New Living Translation
Tyndale House (2013)

TLB The Living Bible
Tyndale House Publishers (1971)

The Voice
Thomas Nelson (2011)

ABOUT THE AUTHOR

Ever since she wrote her first short story in the fourth grade (as a scared little nine year old writing about a nuclear attack during the Cold War) and it was featured front and center on Parents' Night, Audrey-Jane has been told she writes well. She has spent the last eight years in a yearning quest for wisdom and has been asked and encouraged to share, in one place, what she has learned. And so, in God's perfect timing, she has.

She and her husband live in California where, at day's end, they watch from their terrace as the sun slides down the horizon. As lovely as those moments are, their hearts belong to Paris and the French people.

www.findingwisdom.faith